# SHOWING

# *Showing*

## What Pregnancy Tells Us about Being Human

Agnes R. Howard

WILLIAM B. EERDMANS PUBLISHING COMPANY

GRAND RAPIDS, MICHIGAN

Wm. B. Eerdmans Publishing Co.
4035 Park East Court SE, Grand Rapids, Michigan 49546
www.eerdmans.com

26  25  24  23  22  21  20        1  2  3  4  5  6  7

ISBN 978-0-8028-7723-9

**Library of Congress Cataloging-in-Publication Data**

A catalog record for this book is available from the Library of Congress.

To Tal, co-laborer with *eigentliche* and *geistige Kindern*

# Contents

# 1

# *Pregnancy Is How We Got to Be Who We Are*

It's probably reassuring to know that you're not alone in your suddenly peculiar physical condition—you're actually joining millions of other expectant women who are also drooling, vomiting, and waddling their way through their pregnancies.

—WhattoExpect.com (2017)

[T]here is a spiritual reality at work in birth. This should be obvious, given we are speaking of the God-given work of an ensouled body. But, too often, this spiritual reality is not obvious or even acknowledged.

—Susan Windley-Daoust,
*Theology of the Body, Extended* (2014)

E very human being exists because of an event of fertilization and a woman's months-long caregiving to that stranger in utero. Until such time as may bring advanced incubators to take over the job of the womb, this is the means by which humans come to be on the earth. The more we know about fetal development, the more obvious it becomes that a woman's work on behalf of the developing fetus is crucial. Because that work is so important, pregnancy must not be considered narrowly a female concern but broadly a human one, meriting deep reflection and demonstrating goods universal to us as human beings. Pregnancy tells us that embodied generosity is fundamental to human life. Thinking well about pregnancy can help not only childbearing women but also all who surround them to live better together.

When I had just returned from the hospital with my second child, a friend came over to see the baby and, after giving customary praise of the baby's face and temperament, confided that she, too, was expecting. My customary congratulations were met with a grimace: "I love babies, I just hate being pregnant." To be sure, many reasons may explain this "hate being pregnant," from bad timing and grave worries to much more ordinary unhappiness with the discomforts and regulations of pregnancy. Some women love being pregnant but some women have it worse. They have long-running nausea, aches, pains, bloating, and heartburn, plus no drinking and no smoking and no soft cheese, so that complaining about pregnancy is accepted, socially approved if not universal, for American women. "Pregnancy stinks." "I'm so over this." "I just want the baby to come." Discomforts are real, so one hardly should meet negative reports with denial. Still, the cultural currency of those exclamations—*so* over this—neglects something crucial. Conceding that pregnancy can be unpleasant, there must be some way that is not sappy or preachy to recast those expressions. Childbearing troubles need not be denied but should be incorporated into a richer sense of what is going on in this event. We might say pregnancy is a big deal to human beings, not in spite of first-trimester nausea and vomiting but in part because of it. We are the kind of creatures who, in order that any of us come to be, require the conscious care of another human being before we arrive.

How should we talk about pregnancy? Shelves full of books tell what to expect when you are expecting, as do numberless websites, blogs, podcasts, and fetal-tracking apps. Even so, often childbearing is diminished by caricature as a clownish period of bumpy, leaky body parts, by sentimentality, or by dwelling on what can go wrong. This is too low a language for an experience understood, in other times and places, as powerfully near to forces of life and death and to the divine work of crafting new souls. Pregnancy merits serious regard on its own, not just in light of assisted reproductive techniques or rights but in its "normal" occurrence. Every pregnancy is of enormous significance even if it shares much in common with the billions of other such experiences of other women, and indeed shares much with that of billions of other mammals too. This kind of months' long intensive care is a lot to ask one person to give another. Some women might object that it is no trouble at all; some *want* to do this. That may be. Whether or not the work of carrying any particular child is pleasant, this work is prerequisite for human life, and we might as well acknowledge it as such.

In some cases this work is very hard to do, and there are hard parts of it in almost all cases. This work should be honored. Honoring pregnancy well is easier said than done. Some might object to a call for more positive attention to pregnancy on grounds that pregnancy already has been made *too* public. Philosopher Kayley Vernallis makes fair hesitation at moral evaluation of pregnancy—"Are we not already engaged in too much moral scrutiny of childbirth?"—but decides that the practice merits careful appraisal, and that "recognition of courageous childbirth itself requires moral and political courage." Pregnancy sometimes gets honored in ways better to avoid, in mawkish romanticizing of motherhood, or in essentialist stories implying that women are defined by childbearing or inadequate if they do not or cannot bear children. Rejecting all these, this book instead suggests how appreciation of childbearing might proceed from the experience and customs surrounding it.[1]

Understanding childbearing well enriches our sense of who we are as human beings. We are creatures who require generosity, care, and mutual dependence in order to live. This is what we should see when someone walks by with a bump. We should learn to look at this more attentively. Not only pregnant women need to think about pregnancy. This phenomenon is relevant to everyone born. The experience of giving hospitality in the body to another human is not just a useful lesson for women who do it, but for all of us. Indeed, the lesson must be for all of us, lest we settle for clichés that imagine females as givers merely by instinct. The experience of childbearing may be immediate to some women but its implications extend to men too: the hard physical fact that we start in utter dependence on another must temper our predilection for autonomy and independence. The overlap of life, mother to child, is essential to our identity. Your life is an event in the life of another.

All mammals arrive this way. But in a way different from what we presume of other mammals, we are conscious of it and can talk about it. In her writings on reproductive health care, sociologist Barbara Katz Rothman reminds readers that "[w]e are conceived inside of bodies, we come forth after months of hearing voices, feeling the rhythm of the human body, cradled in the pelvic rock of our mothers' walk. . . . That is who we are and how we got to be who we are, not separate beings that must learn to cope with others, but attached beings that must learn how to separate." Thinking well about pregnancy necessarily is part of thinking well about being human, since this is the way each of us appeared. Human beings do not create themselves but come forth out of nurture given by an other. Emphasis on the divine knitting together of the body requires concern for the way that formation happens, the collaboration of those who witness and assist that process. Manners surrounding treatment of pregnant women express the way we value or belittle the work.[2]

Pregnancy powerfully demonstrates the connectedness of human action. In an abstract way we may believe that what we do affects others for good or ill, but the way a pregnant woman provides for and protects the fetus-in-utero illustrates this in a very immediate fashion. The human body knows how to gestate another of its kind without conscious direction, but it takes charity and other virtues to bring forth a child as healthy and ready for birth as possible. Prenatal practices remind a woman, even ingrain in her actions, the awareness that one's doings—standing, falling, fasting, eating, buying, smoking, drinking—immediately affect another person. This mutuality is always true, but it shows through with exceptional obviousness during pregnancy. It is something to see.

## How We Make Babies Now

For middle-class American women, pregnancy looks something like this: A woman might sense that her body feels different—maybe she is nauseated, unusually tired, makes more trips to the bathroom, misses a period—and so she purchases an inexpensive test at a drug store. Applying urine to a plastic stick indicates whether or not a baby is on the way. Thereafter the woman who hopes to have a baby seeks out a birth attendant, usually an obstetrician but sometimes a general practitioner, nurse, or midwife. Initiating prenatal care is a way to express assent that her symptoms mean she will be having a baby. At an initial prenatal visit she is given the calendar day on which the baby is scheduled to appear. Month after month the woman makes prenatal visits, where weight and blood pressure are checked, fetal measurements taken. This sequence of awareness and action is a hallmark of present-day pregnancy. Being pregnant includes *knowing* that you are pregnant, with scientific confirmation. A pregnant woman is supposed to know how pregnancy works and act on that knowledge. She is supposed to take vitamins, avoid some food and drink and take in more of others, stay away from cigarettes and alcohol.

Seeing, as well as knowing, is part of the current experience of pregnancy. American women with wanted pregnancies have ultrasounds, as many as an average of five per pregnancy, according to a recent study. Additional tests and screenings may be ordered too. These can reveal whether the baby has any problems or is developing normally. Ultrasound images also show whether the woman is carrying a boy, girl, twins, or other multiples. Knowing a boy or girl is awaited, parents often announce that fact and the chosen name, ascribing characteristics to the child long before birth.[3]

To coach themselves along through the process women seek out advice, above all from doctors but also from many media sources, guidebooks, magazines, apps, blogs, and chat communities. Most of these guides combine lay-level obstetric counsel with ladies' room gossip: descriptions of the developing fetus at various points, warnings about what not to eat, exclamations over bizarre changes in the body. An expectant mother might also prepare for a baby by taking a class. Classes teach women what might happen in labor and how to survive it, with focus on pain management. Classes additionally might teach breastfeeding and infant-care basics. In a class or on her own, a pregnant woman might do special exercises to prepare for birth and to reclaim her prepregnant figure later.[4]

Complicated or not, coming babies require preparation, which in the United States predominantly means the acquisition of stuff. Minimally this stuff includes maternal items, especially clothes to accommodate the woman's changing shape. Today's maternity outfits no longer conceal the telltale girth but resemble a woman's ordinary clothes. Rather than trying to mask her new figure they flaunt her bump. More merchandise still is sold for the anticipated baby. Expectant parents decorate nurseries, try out cribs, strollers, seats, and carriers, and register for clothes, high chairs, bottles, toys, pacifiers, monitors, feeding implements, and other equipment.[5]

When the due date draws near, the woman may wait for the baby to come on its own time, or be induced, or schedule a cesarean section, most often delivering at a hospital, where doctors and other professionals attend the patient. In the hospital she would be prepped with an IV, may walk around the hallways, get in a tub, and spend some time strapped to a monitor that records the baby's heartbeat. The woman may want the birth to be a meaningful experience or a painless one or sometimes both. She often is offered pain-blocking and labor-accelerating drugs. In many cases she would anticipate bringing forth a healthy newborn, or perhaps a newborn known to require medical care that stands at ready. Parents may script a birth plan to tell what is to be sought or rejected during the process. Given that nearly a third of all American deliveries now are done by cesarean section, it is fairly likely that things will not go according to plan. "Natural" childbirth, usually taken to mean delivery without chemical or mechanical assistance and without pain medication, has appeal but often is set in opposition to hospital techniques that promise more control, less pain, and greater safety.[6] This standard script of American pregnancy and birth is, quite literally, scripted in the many depictions of birth in Hollywood films and cable television series. Though there are variations, particularly on high and low ends of economic scales, this functions as a fair summary of American birth practice now.[7]

## Should Childbearing Be More Natural? Or More Spiritual?

The language of nature sometimes is chosen to describe pregnancy and birth. But very little of the experience described above is merely unadorned nature. Much of what we assume typical, even necessary, about human birth is crafted by culture. Other times and places saw that culture shaped by custom and social expectation and religious belief. Obstetric medicine and consumer buying habits now shape it. Medical sources tell women what is happening during pregnancy, while advertising and popular culture indicate how women are supposed to behave.

Birth overseen by doctors in hospitals with technology assisting can be essential for some women and babies, lifesaving. Still, we should not underestimate how medicine has reshaped birth, an "astounding" transformation, as surgeon Atul Gawande observes, with electronic fetal monitoring, epidural and spinal anesthesia, and labor-accelerating drugs used in high percentages. Gawande sees "something disquieting about the fact that birth is becoming so readily surgical." Birth practices like this have plenty of critics. Some critics charge that medically managed birth treats women like defective machines needing fixing by doctors. Others see a kind of industrial standardization that wrecks birth experiences. Hospital birth is costly. Applying heavy-duty technology and extensive interventions where they are not needed makes the whole undertaking more expensive, a problem in an age of rising medical expenses. The American way of hospital birth offers different services to the poor and to affluent patients. Some critics advocate removal of normal childbirth from medical management in favor of midwifery care.[8]

For others, concerns about doctors and technology in birth are not at base criticism of the use of medicine but its scope. For the obstetrical patient, the experience may involve much more than coming out at the end with a baby in a bassinet: the feeling of having an unknown person growing in one's body; the swelling, blooming, and scarring that accompany expectation; the exhaustion, joy, and surprise that come with the arrival. The complex reactions parents-to-be have to birth and bearing often are incommensurate with a doctor's valuation. This is not necessarily the doctor's fault. A doctor employed to get baby safely out should not necessarily be expected to process the emotional freight patients bring along. But because we have no other common way to capture the significance of pregnancy, we entrust more to the medical realm than perhaps we should. Overextension of medical authority breeds neglect of other interpretations for pregnancy and birth. Though now often marginalized, moral and religious interpretations have in other eras been taken for granted as relevant to birth. Ethicist Michael Banner rues the reduction of birth to medical process, acknowledging that a "challenge, then, for an everyday ethics is to narrate the moral significance or meaning which is or may be found in birth." Because "religious meanings and rites in birthing have themselves been displaced or pushed to the margins by technocratic meaning and rites, those who seek to resist the de-meaning of birth," Banner explains, may not easily find "resources for their resistance" in traditional religion.[9]

Part of the problem too is overemphasis on birth itself, the baby's exit. For the woman involved in the work of childbearing, the big event is not the birth alone but all the months from conception to delivery. Because almost no public means exist to mark this process beyond medical markers—prenatal care, ultrasounds, due-date predictions— too much weight is loaded on the end, where women may be frustrated if delivery goes wrong or departs from the plan. Putting so much emphasis on the birth experience seems almost a guarantor of disappointment. Unlike the birth experience, pregnancy more often gets accorded only private significance, something women may sentimentalize but not something deserving of anyone else's attention—"some kind of narcissistic self-experience in which a woman is merely relating to her body in a novel way," as James Mumford critiques this faulty interpretation. But the woman-with-child is not just relating to her own body. She is relating to another creature inside her body and to her body's response. The long nine-months carry deserves to count as part of the "birth experience," whatever happens when baby actually comes out.[10]

The lack of a culturally current way of appreciating childbearing, outside the medical-scientific one, tends to trivialize an enormously important part of human experience. In a history of pregnancy in Christianity, Anne Stensvold regrets that commentary around the experience now is dominated by "cultural clichés" and private messages, leaving for common use an absence of "words and metaphors which would allow us to reflect and develop our understanding of pregnancy." Though Stensvold faults many responses offered by Christians in the past, her work draws attention to a present-day lack. That lack might be supplied in part through churchly texts and traditions.[11]

We sorely need good "words and metaphors" about pregnancy, words that go beyond the medical and that have broad common currency, words we might access when we think about childbearing. Finding these alternative "scripts" can be a challenge. Hebrew Bible scholar Tikva Frymer-Kensky, packing for the hospital before her first child's birth, took along "two novels, the TV guide and a folder of Mesopotamian birth incantations that I happened to be collecting for my dissertation on water symbolism in Mesopotamia." She found the Mesopotamian texts the most useful, a fact that later angered her: "Why was it, I wanted to know, that I, well-educated in Judaism and in Christianity, had to go all the way back to ancient Babylon in order to find something to read before childbirth? And what could most women do, who do not read Sumerian?"[12]

It is a reasonable question. A believer may *believe* that new life is special, or a gift of God, that God has created each unique, eternal-souled child, or that God "knits together" the fetus, but this understanding dangles loose in private, not readily linked up to the creation story the medical profession offers. More widely accessible theological views of childbearing would be desirable.

To be sure, motherhood books written from religious viewpoints exist aplenty, devotionals for the expectant woman or prayers for the coming child. These can be helpful but carry the implication that religious believers may *opt* to make pregnancy a spiritual event. Pregnancy and birth can carry different spiritual meanings, but meaning inheres in the process rather than only being added by pious parents who wish to celebrate it that way. It is for this reason that better discourse about pregnancy is so important to churches, to those beyond the immediate sphere of parents-to-be. To this end, theologian Susan Windley-Daoust applies Pope John Paul II's theology of the body to birth. She argues that "if the ensouled body *is* a natural and intentional sign, then these realities not only could have meaning, they *do* communicate meaning." A sign points to something beyond itself, to an important reality outside of it, or to God. Windley-Daoust insists "[t]he question is not 'are they meaningful?', but *'what do they mean?'"*

Jesus chose birth as an analogy for the work of redemption, noting that though a laboring woman has pain, she "forgets the anguish because of her joy that a child is born into the world" (John 16:21). The whole creation, wrote the apostle Paul in his letter to the Romans, awaits redemption as though "groaning as in the pains of childbirth" (Rom 8:22). Anne Stensvold, despite her criticism of Christian approaches to childbearing, feels for a nonreligious friend who wants to have a child baptized because "I need to address my gratitude to someone or something." Frymer-Kensky blends her scholarship and birth experience in *Motherprayer*, a compilation of writings from various religions' traditions made accessible to women unable to read Sumerian. Lutheran minister Margaret Hammer, struck by the "preponderance of religious expressions parents used to describe their child's birth" even among putatively nonreligious people, wonders, "Can the church offer parents anything that they cannot find elsewhere amid the mounds of literature, and wealth of workshops and classes? Conversely, will the church gain anything important by focusing more attention on the experience of giving birth? In a word—yes!"[13]

Yes indeed. Though in a tradition as rich with reflection on creation, the body, and the family as Western Christianity, what is to be found on childbearing sometimes feels thinner than what might be wanted. As Stephanie Paulsell recognizes, Christianity offers an "ambiguous legacy" on this count, offering traditions honoring the body but also uneasiness about it. Theologians centuries ago certainly took an interest in how babies came to be. In the early church and Middle Ages, at a very high level theologians pondered conception to understand Mary and the incarnation. On a plane only slightly less ethereal, they wondered how God placed a soul into each forming body. In consideration of actual women, the reasons that pregnancy came under church scrutiny restricted the kind of scrutiny it got. In best cases, an attitude that could be called modesty discouraged too much searching under women's skirts. In suspicious cases, a swelling belly might be of interest as evidence of illicit sex, done with the wrong person or at the wrong time. Women who lost pregnancies might be queried about intent to abort. During witchcraft panics, pregnant women drew suspicion for physical dalliance with demons. With a kind of discouraging regularity, inquiry into the way theologians before modern times thought about pregnancy turns up these kinds of issues. Some critics of Christianity see this dismal attitude as part of a whole regrettable cloth, just the way Western Christianity derogates women. This judgment errs too. Devotional practices and veneration of saints through the Middle Ages carry evidence that feminine spirituality did not go unappreciated. Still, Christian traditions and theology neglect many opportunities to appreciate the everyday miracle of woman with child. "It is striking to me that there is so very little written on a theology of birth," admits Windley-Daoust, work left "scandalously" undone even as she credits recent writers with strides made in this direction. In terms of pregnancy, a religiously informed way of honoring the body needs to be "excavated," to use Paulsell's terms, and needs to be "put in dialogue" with other contemporary considerations.[14]

The thinness of theological resources from some periods does not mean that none exist. Hammer rues that "theologians have treated the experience of birth warily, sketchily, and haphazardly, if at all," perhaps because of the "very femaleness of this experience," leading birth to be "perceived as a special interest topic." Readers, take note: childbearing is not just a special-interest topic. In the sixteenth and seventeenth centuries, responding to new patterns of piety and literacy, Protestant and Catholic men offered devotional books for mothers and families that sometimes praised physical and spiritual features of childbearing. In the eighteenth and nineteenth centuries, when motherhood got much sentimental treatment, the self-sacrifice and piety of expectant women received abundant attention. Beyond those materials, theologians in our own time seek to show how Scripture and tradition can be applied fruitfully to childbearing. Some writers reflect on the Hebrew Bible's imagery of God as birthing or nursing mother, on the paradox of the incarnation, on the travail and delivery in the Gospels. The Christian tradition offers a vocabulary adequate to the profundity of bearing and birthing, a story connecting creation, suffering and joy, and a respect for the integrity and dignity of the human person, body and soul. Considering birth in those terms offers the church and the world better insight into the nature of God and human possibility, our relationships to each other, our responsibilities for each other.[15]

A great deal may be gained by cultivating some voice beyond the medical one to help answer the questions, big and small, that arise in childbearing. Why does carrying around another person make a pregnant woman throw up? Loathe her favorite food? Why does pregnancy make once-straight hair curly? Inscribe a dark line down the belly?

"Hormones" is not a sufficient answer. Even more pressing are questions about the relationship of mother and other: who is this unseen character in utero, and who does the woman become while walking around with (at least) two bodies, two heads, two souls, enclosed in the space of one?

To build a bridge between consideration of pregnancy as a strictly medical thing or as a moral and spiritual experience, we may weave together theologically inflected counsel with the layperson's medical script, prenatal care guides. What-to-expect books, especially old ones, give much more than menus and exercises. Prenatal care manuals can underwrite common reflection about pregnancy. They help link the medical to human experience beyond it. Interpretation of these instruction manuals even can give tools to help see pregnancy for what it is, meaningful work shaping a woman's habits even as she helps shape the fetus. Pregnant women are given many commands. Take your vitamins, or the baby might have neural tube defects. Put down that glass of wine, or the child may suffer low birth weight. Don't empty that cat-litter box, or the baby might have brain or vision problems. Sleep on your left side, or you might slow blood circulation to the fetal body. The behaviors pregnant women are expected to adopt call for practice of what we might call virtue, though it is rarely acknowledged as such. This is most emphatically *not* to say that pregnancy itself is virtue. But pregnancy gives distinct opportunity for the practice of virtues, a description that might be claimed by the mother herself and by others who have chance to observe it.

Because pregnancy becomes a visible condition, and because familiarity with fetal images encourages passersby to make connections between what a pregnant woman is doing and how the baby is becoming, the public at large shares assumptions that a woman's behavior has immediate bearing on the good of that new person. This recognition is important for the mother and also for onlookers, that women do *this* in order that we all come to exist. The pregnant woman you pass on the street is not just doing what women always have done. The contrast between the way pregnancy used to be lived and what we now judge as normal may help us to recognize how and why pregnancy deserves a more substantive appraisal. That is another source from which we might draw a rich understanding of pregnancy that can be made serviceable and common: historical reflection. History of childbearing sometimes gets mined for strange-but-true tidbits about how women were misunderstood or abused through weird potions or brutal births. That usage is unfortunate, because considering how pregnancy was handled and discussed in the past, even where peculiar, can enhance our own practice and understanding.

## How We Used to Make Babies

The experience of a pregnant woman in the United States until comparatively recently—say, a century and a half ago—looked very different. That experience resembled the experience of women across earlier centuries perhaps more than it felt like our own. To begin, there was no beginning, at least not a clear one. The pregnant woman would not know she was pregnant for a long way into the process. There was no sure way in early months to certify whether pregnancy or something else, ill health or upset stomach, was causing her discomfort. Therefore she would have no cause in this period to behave any differently from her ordinary ways in terms of diet, labor, sociability, or risk. Only the symptoms of several months' duration could confirm pregnancy.

While her reproductive capacities were understood as a great part of her reason for being female, she was not presumed to be doing very much in making a baby. Ancient theories of reproduction, disputed but not uprooted until well into the nineteenth century, taught that the father's "seed" made the baby, that the woman provided merely material stuff and an environment for the father's offspring to grow. Aristotle (384–322 BCE) argued that male seed was the immaterial means of creating a child. Only men had seed that made a new being. Galen (129–216 CE) in contrast argued that men and women both had seed that mixed to make a child, though women's seed tended to be weaker. Through the Middle Ages these views were blended and referenced far into the early modern period in Europe and America. Neither the pregnant woman nor anyone else could see what the baby looked like, or whether a boy or girl was on the way. The best proof she could have that a baby existed at all was her perception of its movement at about four months. The baby's movement, its "quickening," told her and others that what stretched out her abdomen was a living being. As the woman grew larger and anticipated birth, she might begin a period of confinement lasting through the baby's arrival—no one could tell exactly when that might be—and for several weeks after. Well into the twentieth century, most women would deliver babies at home, with doctor, nurse, or midwife to help.[16]

The point of highlighting contrasts between past views and practices of childbearing and current ones is not to congratulate ourselves on knowing something our ancestors did not. Nor is it to suggest that old ways were somehow more truthful about reproduction than our current beliefs and practices. Instead, the disparities between current and former understandings underscore pregnancy as a culturally shaped rather than an eternally-same biological process. Above all we see that the odd old ways were directed to mysteries that remain mysterious. Despite medicine's enhanced understanding, aspects of childbirth that remain beyond our control demand explanation in a humane way, not just a scientific way. What was puzzling or misunderstood in the past might help us to use what we know now to better effect. Contrast with former views also might help us skirt the error of believing we understand all that is necessary, since there is a great deal that remains opaque and later scientific developments may make our own views seem naïve.

For all the absurdity of some old views, these approaches to childbearing were on target in other respects. First, they recognized the gravity of childbearing, an event that could hurt or even kill the mother. For us, thankfully, death in childbirth is rare and pain can be muted, but absenting mortal danger, we are left on our own to explain why the experience is meaningful. Second, the gravity of the occasion helped affirm that birth possessed spiritual significance, so divine presence and prayers were presumed appropriate in childbed. Third, concession to the mystery of baby-making—why a child was male or female, had some parental traits and not others, had intact features or not—generated reflection and wonder.[17]

Our up-to-date knowledge about pregnancy and fetal development already should have improved the way we discuss childbearing. Maybe it has in some ways. Old views of pregnancy we can dismiss, but many of our current views also miss the mark. Recognition that mother's behavior affects the fetus often skips right over appreciation to throw blame on her if something goes wrong. Women can underappreciate childbearing, as though praising pregnancy might risk implication that motherhood should be a woman's chief or only calling. And women emphasizing the "naturalness" of childbearing can downplay its gravity as they stress healthy normalcy, lest bringing forth life be deemed a pathology needing medical intervention.

The fact that so many protocols of pregnancy now are different from those in the past might pique curiosity about what was behind the older views. Philosophers, doctors, and religious figures who lacked our knowledge of biology puzzled over procreation, wondered why human beings emerged the way they did. On the outside, a pregnant woman was becoming visibly different, both more than her ordinary self and also unlike her ordinary self. On the inside she was doing a work both mysterious and manifest, and therefore in some ways instructive—maybe even rehearsing the creation of the world. Kathleen Crowther-Heyck's analysis of guides for early modern women in Germany finds that for sixteenth-century writers, "the processes of generation in the womb mirrored the processes of generation in the larger world. This analogy was part of a worldview that linked the macrocosm—the greater world—and the microcosm—man." Because medical writers and pastors alike compared pregnancy to the whole work of creation writ small, these writers saw that the "analogical relationship between the womb and the world lent enormous symbolic significance and religious meaning to the processes of conception, pregnancy, and birth."[18]

Men and women in earlier times, with what looks to us primitive science, asked some good questions about childbearing. Old questions and answers might be employed to plumb more deeply the explanations science currently provides. Within our much more sophisticated understanding of gestation, we might still ask other questions. Since we know enough about the effects of the maternal body on the developing fetus to require action on the part of the woman, what goods might we appreciate in her behavior? What about the experience of pregnancy do we hope is formative for the mother, a life experience comprehensible to her and to others around her? How might observation of her nurture shape others around her? How do the cultural practices we expect of mothers help us recognize praiseworthy features of human life through the biology of pregnancy? The benefits of the way human beings bring forth children are not valuable only to those particular children, but to us in general, especially if we understand them as goods.

To approach those questions, this book makes use of manuals that told previous generations what to expect when they were expecting. Some of these come from centuries ago, and others from the early to middle twentieth century, a heyday for prenatal advice-giving. While these guides give some advice we now deem flatly wrong, their preoccupations and counsels help us to do two things better. First, we see how old attitudes changed (or not) as scientific and medical practice changed. Second, we see, through the scripting of maternity habits in terms strange to us, the way that childbearing might be estimated now as active on the mother's part, caring and purposeful. Reference to the old guides allows a kind of archaeology of the way our pregnancy culture emerged and a reflection on how we might do better.

## How This Book Reconsiders Childbearing

Pregnancy can be interpreted through many lenses, biology or anthropology or evolutionary development, telling "what it means" in those terms. But for my purposes here, traditions and practices help to tell "what it means"—what presumed experts had to say about pregnant women and what they advised women to do. Prenatal care tells us what pregnancy is supposed to be like and why it matters. When a pregnant woman passes beyond the point when her condition can be concealed behind clothes, we say she is "showing." She *is* showing: in her actions and physical changes, the pregnant woman is showing some nonnegotiable facts of human life—our reliance on relationship, generosity, and physical presence. These goods are crucial in individual lives. And collectively we recognize these goods as ideal for the continuation of human life. We flourish by doing these things.

Much has been written about reproduction. But if some writing from the remote past suffered from one kind of blind spot, that from the present suffers from another. Premodern people managed to fix the fetus in their sights and obscure the maternal body. As Irina Aristarkhova puts it, "[e]mbryology, until very recently, has dealt with only one part of generation, with the 'embryo.'" More recent misconceptions are built on traditional ones. Explanations begun this way focus on how the baby grows, how the baby gets out—not what it is like for a woman to be doing this. Aristarkhova concludes, "The fact that human pregnancy is so much about the mother and her body is not yet accounted for in biomedical sciences. This disregard involves a fundamental misunderstanding of the full potential of the maternal-fetal interface and the interaction it enables."[19]

This book is not a hearts-and-flowers tribute to motherhood. That Victorian caricature distorts the importance of pregnancy and should be avoided. But it would be wrong too to shrink from appraising pregnancy positively in order to avoid those mistakes about what woman can do or be. To argue that looking at pregnancy tells us something important can cause pain to some, I recognize, perhaps especially to those who have experienced infertility or pregnancy loss. Some may have plenty of reasons not to wish any more sustained gaze at pregnancy. I recognize—and regret—ways that positive appraisal of childbearing can exacerbate that pain. That difficulty, though, also attests to the claim this book makes, that childbearing carries meaning not only for current parents-to-be but for church and community more broadly. Infertility deserves respectful treatment, though like many of the maternity manuals used here as primary sources, these pages cannot do justice to the topic.

Developing a better view of the moral work of carrying a baby begins with an understanding of past theories and practices, then goes to investigation of ways the pregnant woman acts for good. The focus in this book as a whole is specific to childbearing culture in the United States, as birth practices differ somewhat even in countries like our own in other respects. To get at American experience in our own time requires some looking backward into the European history of ideas and practices surrounding reproduction. Chapter two offers a short sketch of a long stretch of history of embryology and birth. The "seed" theories of Aristotle and Galen, early modern adjustments of these systems, medieval church teaching on fetal ensoulment, propositions of preformation that emerged out of what seventeenth-century microscopes revealed, and the cascade of insights from nineteenth-century science: all these bore implications for women while pregnant. This history provides foundation for the birth practices many Americans now take for granted. The shift from home to hospital births runs parallel to the shift from midwifery care to that proffered by obstetricians. Our culture of birth has been shaped not only by experts but by popular patterns, like the management of cravings, morning-sickness remedies, maternity clothing, and rituals for lying-in.

The chapters that follow then provide normative interpretation of childbearing, analyzing the character of the work. Chapter three outlines what women are doing and demonstrating in carrying a child. Knowledge of fetal development spurs women to be aware that their behavior affects the fetus and makes others expect women to behave appropriately. This awareness—a woman's own and others'—of what she is doing is an important feature of pregnancy, one that distinguishes the experience now from what being pregnant in other times and places would be like. Two distinguishing features of pregnancy in our time, that women can know they are pregnant and that we know how the fetus develops, dramatically change the experience. A woman serves as a witness in two ways: first as one who witnesses in a unique way the formation of a new person, and second as one who shows others what is involved in bearing life.

Chapter four focuses on the most basic goods women give the fetus-in-utero, protection and provision. Providing nutrients for the baby has been understood from antiquity as a mother's duty. More than eating for two, the job of planning, ingesting, and digesting the right stuff can make all the difference in fetal development. Keeping the fetus safe, sheltered, and nourished can be demanding work. The ways that pregnancy practices differ so sharply from ordinary life, and the fact that carrying a baby sometimes can endanger the mother, allows attention to virtue.

Chapter five defines key components of maternity in the vocabulary of virtue, especially prudence, courage, hope, charity, and hospitality. The premise here is not that the plain biology of pregnancy equals virtue. Rather, the woman's situation allows for the development of some good habits and dispositions, treated here in language some philosophers name as virtues. For instance, with prudence an expectant woman evaluates how the fetus develops and how she might equip herself to provide necessary things. Courage and hope are engaged in a mother's faithful care in the face of dangers that dog pregnancy and birth. Charity and hospitality orient a woman to seek the good for the developing child as she moderates her own requirements to accommodate a guest.

Chapter six considers how the presence of the fetus alters the pregnant woman herself. In some respects her identity in the body is blurred, in the body's appearance and its singular character. Anticipation of future motherhood also reshuffles identity. The maternal body keeps evidence of the child borne. A woman's pregnancy may alter relationships, with the fetus, with the father of the child, with family and community of whom she will expect things on a baby's behalf.

The conclusion makes proposals about ways American culture and churches might better honor these labors and transformations of childbearing. Prenatal care can describe the nurture a woman gives to a fetus, but also the way others support a woman in that work. In the realm of manners we might shift, even a little, to express common appreciation of a necessary human work.

Here a clarification is in order about terminology and my way of addressing pregnancy. In general I try to call a pregnant woman and a fetus by those names, though to reduce redundancy and allow variety as well as to honor shades of meaning, woman is sometimes also called "mother," "expectant woman," "mother-to-be," and the fetus sometimes gets named "baby," "coming child," or, with credit to James Mumford, "newone." I recognize that these terms are not casually interchangeable. I recognize the many distinctions readers might apply to distinguish them, especially refusal to call a woman "mother" until she chooses that name, or call the fetus "baby" or "child" until the woman permits that label. I uphold this usage despite these complexities, perhaps primarily because in doing so I am following conventions of maternity manuals themselves. While principled distinctions may be upheld between fetus and baby in philosophical discussion or in abortion polemics, the distinction is almost entirely absent in prenatal manuals. Prenatal care guides for women routinely name the fetus "baby" and assume that the woman reading the guides, whom they often address as "mom," will do so too. The genre of maternity advice manuals presupposes both that this is appropriate usage and that their readership will agree. In any case, books written to counsel expectant women on how to care for themselves before baby arrives consistently behave as though the reader is an expectant mother who thinks about the creature resulting from her pregnancy as a baby, and who wants to read and talk about the creature as such. Of course this is not true of all readers or all pregnancies. But the sorts of sources marked here as especially instructive presuppose the possibility of addressing women this way.

Furthermore, I recognize that pregnancies of individual women can differ in almost every possible way, perhaps most fundamentally in a woman's intent or desire to be pregnant and in her decision to carry through the pregnancy to term. This book observes those limits and others, not claiming to address all variations that race, ethnicity, class, and social circumstance may impose. It may seem arrogant to be telling any other woman, let alone people in general, what any pregnancy "means." That undertaking I attempt nevertheless, because a shared sense of the nature of this human experience is generally needful and also may be useful to an individual—even by provoking dissent from my views of what it "means." Maternity guides tell women to do this, that, and the other. I puzzle over what good comes, what habits are shaped, by this, that, and the other. Even objection to these chapters as a shared script may, in part, underscore the need for such a thing and could facilitate development of a better one.

# 2

# *How We Used to Make Babies*

So miraculous did primitive peoples consider this phenomenon that they ascribed it all to superhuman intervention. . . . but now we know that pregnancy comes about in only one way: from the union of a female germ cell, the egg or ovum, with a male germ cell, the spermatozoon.

—Nicholson J. Eastman, *Expectant Motherhood* (1957)

Pregnancy, childbirth, and the puerperium wear thin the veneer of civilization.

—Stuart B. Blakely, "Superstitions in Obstetrics" (1922)

For centuries pregnant women suffering from heartburn believed this discomfort signaled that their babies would be born with a fuller head of hair. In the twentieth century, doctors dismissed those old wives' tales and encouraged mothers-to-be instead to avoid rich or spicy foods. Curious about the superstition's persistence into the early twenty-first century, Johns Hopkins researcher Kathleen Costigan and her colleagues studied expectant mothers complaining of heartburn and discovered that they actually did bear hairy babies. This was a surprise. "Contrary to expectations, it appears that an association between heartburn severity during pregnancy and newborn hair does exist," the researchers announce in their 2006 study. Costigan concedes that when she heard this claim before, "I've always told people it's nonsense," but now she "had to eat a lot of crow." Why does heartburn indicate hair? Hormones. As with other symptoms of pregnancy that might seem to require cosmic explanation, the medical answer for this discomfort is that god-in-the-machine, hormones—an answer armored with the prestige of science but flimsy in linking human experience with outcomes.[1]

Costigan and colleagues write that "Folklore can originate by detection of actual associations between seemingly unrelated events and [be] perpetuated through oral tradition." That is, the belief apparently arose because women detected some connection between heartburn and big hair and passed this information down, mother to daughter, until professionals told them to stop believing that nonsense. Explaining pregnancy discomforts in terms of hormones, the researchers instead "propose a shared biologic mechanism involving a dual role of pregnancy hormones in both the relaxation of the lower esophageal sphincter and the modulation of fetal hair growth." It is not that heartburn *causes* hair but that hormones cause both, the former serving merely as a marker rather than a cause of the latter.[2]

The moral of this story is not that superstitions should be revived or that medicine is wrong. The point is that so important a human phenomenon as pregnancy deserves humane reflection, but this reflection has been muted by treating pregnancy as a mostly medical condition. Because medicine sent superstitions packing generations ago, other explanations of pregnancy from folklore or custom or religious tradition now are too far out of reach for most people to avail. When, in the case of heartburn, antique conviction fails to melt beneath scientific scrutiny, we still look to medicine to give meaning. Thus we now say that pregnant women feeling heartburn might predict a hairy infant because the hormones tell them so. In place of customary explanation, "hormones" act as a placeholder suggesting there is no *story* to this funny thing, just the working out of scientific fact.

A brief look at antique convictions about pregnancy can be helpful in recalling what puzzled others. People have not always thought about the body as we do: separate from other creatures and the environment around us, determined by genes and volition, amenable to chemical manipulation. If the aim of this chapter were properly a history of ideas about reproduction, orderly procession would be made from the ancient Greeks through medieval philosophy and Renaissance medicine, Scientific Revolution, and on up. But the job of this section is not predominantly to lay out that long and fascinating narrative, a task already handled by a number of fine books. Instead of a formal history of science, this chapter takes as its starting point the way Americans now perceive pregnancy and then backs into older understandings of the same things. We know that sperm plus egg makes baby. Therefore we want to recall here how others used to understand sperm, egg, and resultant baby. This history is put to service, excavating resolved but still provocative questions about reproduction that have been covered over by current practice.[3]

Past theorists assumed some things substantially different from our reproductive assumptions. (In the text that follows, these people will sometimes be called scientists or doctors, anachronistic labels but helpful in categorizing them, and others will be called philosophers or theologians.) Many in this range of thinkers assumed that men and women had comparable organs with different degrees of completeness, that a man delivered seed to the womb of a woman where it would receive nutrients and warmth and, if the planets were aligned and the woman did not disrupt the growth, at the end a midwife might help bring to birth the resulting baby. This chapter proceeds in that order, first noting some older views of the body, then of the "seed," then of the embryo and fetus, going finally to birth and its attendants.

If we suspend conviction for a few pages that we know how babies are made—sperm plus egg, two lines, nine months, and an epidural— much of the course to a baby's arrival is more evidently mysterious. Why are male and female bodies the way they are? Even as we accept what X and Y chromosomes dictate, plenty is left to figure out about male and female. How does their coupling produce a child? This too is still a good question, especially as the preferential option of our own sexual norms is explicitly intended *not* to produce a child.[4]

Holding aside the sperm-egg-birth story allows lists of reasonable questions to surface, questions that long shaped European and American thought about reproduction. For instance:

- What does each parent contribute to the formation of a child?
- How does a baby's body grow from a fluid blob into solid, articulated parts?

- Why does a child resemble her parents, or not?
- What obligations do childbearing women have to self, spouse, offspring, community?
- What obligations does a community have to childbearing women?
- And the big one, the one that lies just underneath many of the others: Why do things go wrong, miscarriages, diseases, anomalies?

For the most part in the United States we take these as settled questions rather than disputed ones because the medical profession has done so much to supply the answers. Treading carefully is crucial in discussing the rise of obstetrics. It is hard to say almost anything about the history of doctor-managed birth without seeming to choose sides, doctors over midwives or vice versa. The obstetric profession in the United States did rise in part through active suppression of midwives, though some obstetricians supported nurse-midwifery. While many physicians past and present doubtless sought the best interests of women and children, the transition from midwifery at home to doctor-supervised birth had winners and losers. Establishing obstetrics as the birth authority of first and last resort shaped a new culture of pregnancy, in which the body is explained in terms of diagnoses and symptoms, problems are raised and resolved in examination rooms, and confidence is kept between a woman and her doctor. The rise of obstetrics as the authority for childbearing depended substantially on eliminating or displacing mystery. Birth increasingly seemed to *require* medical expertise as doctors detailed all that could go wrong; bodies and births should be entrusted to those skillful enough to handle them.

Others over time have found quite different meanings in pregnancy and birth. Contrasting current attitudes with childbearing in sixteenth-century Germany, Ulinka Rublack observes that in "developed countries today, pregnancy and miscarriage, birth and death, are seldom thought to be 'rich with meanings which penetrate the whole of social life,'" as they were understood by early modern people. Some old ideas and practices deserve rejection, but some that we have rejected answered real human needs and have been replaced with no adequate substitute. In the 1960s Yale medical historian Thomas Rogers Forbes mused that "[r]eproductive phenomena have puzzled mankind since very early times. . . . man must always wonder where he came from and how he was produced." Forbes conceded in his own time that these phenomena were "mysteries still partly unsolved," and often the "accepted belief of one age may be rejected as nonsense in the next." Outmoded beliefs need not only be reckoned as nonsense but also as a useful record of ways other people have confronted mysteries yet unsolved.[5]

## The Male and Female Body

The way we understand the body shapes the way we live in it, as it did for people in the past. People in previous eras did not think of their ideas as oddball explanations for natural phenomena because they could come up with no better answers, but credited their understandings no less than we do our own. Reviewing old ideas of reproduction requires starting with old ideas about male and female bodies. What you think you are going to see shapes what you see. That is, an assumption that women are weak or deformed can lead people to look for features of females that seem weak, and then "discovery" of weakness gets encoded into law and custom. In general, male writers in old Western texts recognized the male body as the perfect or ideal or complete human form, while they described the female as less powerful or less developed.[6]

Ideas from ancient Greece shaped the way many people in Europe viewed males and females for a long time. Old models of bodies and theories of reproduction were compiled, repackaged, and reprinted over and over across centuries. For instance, the influential 1513 manual of Eucharius Rösslin (ca. 1470–ca. 1526), *Rosegarden for Pregnant Women and Midwives,* patched together Greek texts from the Hippocratic corpus, plus Galen, medieval writings from Avicenna (980–1037) and Albert the Great (ca. 1200–1280), and added more contemporary texts, mostly from Italian physician Michele Savonarola (ca. 1385–1466). This conglomeration subsequently was carried into other languages and reprinted often.[7]

Sometimes anatomical models carried over from ancient texts into each generation's canon contradicted one another but were nevertheless transmitted together as valid. Old views about sex and bodies persisted in high and popular opinion for centuries. One historian declares that there was "no systematic reproductive biology, not even among learned people" into the Middle Ages and beyond. Furthermore, classical ideas about the body influenced popular texts and also reached those who could not read, as they cropped up in stories, dramas, home remedies, and jokes. Accretion of old reproductive ideas eventually shaped American views too.[8]

To be sure, views of the body changed a great deal across the many centuries so blithely lumped together here. Historians mark turning points with the 1540s publication of Renaissance anatomy texts by Andreas Vesalius (1514–1564) emerging from his study and dissections; with Enlightenment emphases on matter and scientific methods; with eighteenth- and nineteenth-century classification of women by their reproductive capacities; and, of course, with the progress made more recently in endocrinology, genetics, and fetal imaging. What is striking, though, is how long antique judgments about female bodies and generation perdured, residual assumptions undergirding culture of pregnancy even as the science of it moved on—so powerfully that as late as the twentieth century a distinguished physician could describe a fertilized ovum as having "fresh life impressed on it by impregnation," using a phrase that could have come straight from ancient Greece.[9]

While some thinkers in the nineteenth century treated reproductive organs as women's most salient feature, for ancient Greeks, women's purported inability to reproduce was the very hallmark of their sex. "The woman is as it were a misbegotten man," goes the familiar definition of Aristotle, sometimes otherwise translated as "mutilated" or "infertile" or "defective" male. Writings about the human body from medical traditions associated with Hippocrates (ca. 460–370 BCE) described four "humors," blood, bile, black bile, and phlegm, with health found in the balance of them. Men were more hot and dry, women more cold and moist. Female bodies were described as spongy with superfluous fluids that could be emitted as menstrual blood or transformed into milk. Galen imagined maleness and femaleness along a continuum, developing ideas from Hippocrates to explain the reproductive organs of each sex as homologous. That is, in his view male and female sex organs were basically the same, except that women's insufficient heat left their important parts on the inside of the body rather than allowing them to emerge fully developed on the outside, uterus comparable to scrotum, female "testes" like male testes.

Even later anatomists often still considered female organs in terms of their equivalent in the male. Robert Barret in 1699, describing the "Instruments of Generation in Women," began with "the Spermatick

Preparatory Vessels; some of which agree pretty much with those in Men." While it was clear to all that woman actually bore forth babies, the father was counted the parent. Aeschylus (525/524–456/455 BCE) narrates the arrangement in his drama *Eumenides*: "The woman you call the mother of the child/is not the parent, just a nurse to the seed,/ the new-sown seed that grows and swells inside her./The man is the source of life."[10]

Aristotle disagreed with those who claimed that women were merely containers for reproduction, instead insisting that women provided the matter needed for making a baby. He concurred that women had less heat, indeed, he thought women's heat inadequate to bring digestion to its conclusion to produce "seed," or semen, at all. Aristotle sharpened the distinctions between the sexes, envisioning the woman as opposite to the man, his the complete human body, hers the imperfect. Scientists following Galen assumed men and women were basically the same rather than two distinct kinds of beings. Historian Thomas Laqueur calls this assumption a one-sex model; though scholars debate the specifics of this model's predominance, it was influential and persistent.[11]

When Christian thinkers in the past tried to incorporate these conceptions of body and sex, some disputed points required wrestling through. The science of ancient Greece established understandings of reproduction that were carried over substantially into Christian Europe, even as revisions and confusions were added. Clarissa Atkinson argues that "Church Fathers did not design a program for Christian mothers or write handbooks of obstetrics, gynecology, or infant care," but adapted classical ideas as needed. Could woman's supposedly misbegotten body, for instance, fit in a creation by a God who would not make a mistake? Thomas Aquinas resolved that difficulty in the thirteenth century, explaining that while an individual woman herself may be defective in body, in the context of humans as a whole hers was no defect but a necessity for generation. That solution made its way into midwifery manuals explaining that "almighty God had so institute[d] that women should be the vessels wherein the seed of mankind should be conceived. . . . Nature created the womb or matrix to be the said receptacle wherein she mought [sic] at her leisure work her divine feats about the seed once conceived." Because the "privy works of God" arranged generation to work the way it did, even though seemingly inferior, the female body could not be called defective.[12]

Christian inquiry into reproduction sometimes sought to discern God's aims in the making of male and female and new life, though often these debates arose around theological points rather than abstract ones. Interest in ordinary reproduction sprouted from interest in the extraordinary birth of Jesus. Catholic and later Protestant physicians and theologians sought to understand the timing of conception and the process of ensoulment, in part to follow to logical conclusions doctrines of original sin (why Martin Luther maintained that the soul came from the father, passing down guilt of first parents) and predestination (John Calvin's keen interest on God's foreknowledge respecting the embryo). Stakes were high in these complex deliberations, their gravity admirable.

But at points, the spirit behind these arguments might strike even a reader from within those religious traditions as discouraging. The motive seldom seems to be curiosity about how to name the mystery of living as a body enclosing another body, or pastoral concern to encourage women in that work. Instead accurate assessment of sin seems to drive a lot of disputation, discerning how much iniquity held in particular cases of fornication, adultery, or potential infanticide. The timing of conception and fetal development were of interest less by themselves than as tools to reveal the degree and kind of a woman's sin in abortion or in illegitimate sexual contact. Thus a claim that the fetus is ensouled at conception immediately translates into sanctions against early abortion, rather than pausing to delight in woman's presence at the divine work. An eighteenth-century text titled *Sacred Embryology* has almost nothing to say about a woman's faithful carriage of a child to term but parses the moral obligation of saving woman or child when delivery threatens both lives. Positive evaluation of motherhood and birth exist as well, but the theological tradition is limited by comparatively heavy stress on sin at the expense of awe over generation.[13]

Two points about old views of male and female should be stressed before attending to the actual making of babies. First, most inquiry into the making of a baby assumed that the woman's body could not do very much. The man's action made the baby while the woman was by and large passive. Second, even where activity was ascribed to women it was not understood as volitional but mostly outside their control. The tendency of the uterus to grow, move, and change shape gave the organ an outsized reputation in positive and negative ways. Folk understanding embroidered theories of Plato or Hippocrates to imagine the so-called "wandering womb" like an animal that could move through the body and craved male seed, greedily grabbing at it. The womb was thought to roam, swell, even choke the woman. Jacques Gélis lists some of the metaphors applied to the uterus: "pod, pocket, horn or botte; black hole, swere, place of darkness and horror; mother, anchorage or fertile field of nature. . . . the magic crucible . . . the secret place which is the source of life." The exploits of this very active organ were beyond the woman's sway. Significant bits of baby-making came from the male.[14]

*Seed*

Galen and some others thought men and women both made seed. Aristotle maintained that only men did so. Premodern scientists sought to describe what this fluid was, how it was formed in a man's body, and how it caused a baby. Some guessed that the seed came from the brain and traveled through the marrow, others that seed gathered contributions from all parts of the father's frame and presented that supply of what made arms, legs, head, heart, to the gestator. Hippocrates suggested that the whole body secreted seed "from the hard parts as well as the soft and from the total bodily fluid." We ought not nod recognition too quickly at this term "seed," as though familiar to us, as though the ancient usage were just a quaint agricultural label for what we now call sperm, semen, or egg. Male seed was fluid, white, and frothy because of what it was thought to be. Aristotle described seed as *not* material but a fully concocted essence purified from the blood, a kind of final distillation of nutriment by which a man could generate another human being. Women were thought to have trouble digesting or "concocting" their intake thoroughly, or did not have enough heat to do the job. Thus Aristotle denied that women had seed but ascribed to them its equivalent, blood expelled with menstruation. The woman contributed the matter to the fetus and man contributed the form, which effected a new human soul. A common metaphor likened the male to a sculptor shaping something out of the material, stone or wood, that the female provided. The seed's effect could also be compared to rennet on milk, "curdling" the fetal body like cheese, a metaphor also used by the prophet Job, asking whether God did not "pour me out like milk and curdle me like cheese" (10:10).[15]

For centuries in Europe, texts combined Galen's two-seed theory with Aristotelian accounts of how the seed worked. In the Middle Ages Albert the Great, German teacher and bishop, ascribed to women the task of fermenting the seed. Albert's student Thomas Aquinas (1225–1274) reinforced Aristotle's explanation though attributing to God the infusion of a human soul. Thomas thought the force that made the living embryo grow "is in the semen, and which is derived from the soul of the generator, is, as it were, a certain movement of this soul itself. . . . based on the (vital) spirit in the semen which is frothy."[16]

Whip-tailed, DNA-bearing gametes swimming in a fluid base were not what ancients had in mind when they contemplated seed. It was a shock when late seventeenth-century experiments viewing semen under microscopes revealed spermatozoa. Anton van Leeuwenhoek (1632–1725) gets credit for what he discovered about the cellular reality of human "seed," though in tight competition with other scientists. Examining his own under a microscope Leeuwenhoek found it to be teeming with "animalcules." Some judged these to be worms or parasites that had gotten into the fluid; Leeuwenhoek intuited that they were crucial to reproduction. His contemporary Nicolaas Hartsoeker (1656–1725) famously rendered a little man curled up in the head of a sperm, homunculus in a bubble.[17]

## Egg

Like the Northwest Passage or intelligent life in outer space, the human egg long inspired ardent searching by those sure of its existence and by those persuaded of its impossibility. For us the egg is obvious, ovum, the female counterpart of sperm, the sex cell, the female seed. Ancient seekers found that equivalency not obvious at all. Aristotle and adherents of his embryology saw no need for it. Some thought it could not exist. Two-seed theorists like Galen deemed fluid from the "female testes" the woman's version of semen. Following Galen, persistent Western belief that female orgasm was prerequisite to conception rested on the hypothesis that she needed to emit seed and add movement and heat to set the embryo. A sixteenth-century English guide agreed with Galen both that women had seed and that hers was inferior to that from males, "weak, fluey, cold, and moist," it was "nothing so firm, perfect, absolute, and mighty in a woman as in a man,"—though the writer refused to call this an imperfection. It was simply the nature of woman. Well into the seventeenth century theorists debated whether a female contribution to the embryo even was necessary. Some anatomists by then, comparing humans to other animals, did grow convinced that women must have some sort of egg.[18]

English scientist William Harvey (1578–1657), royal physician to Charles I and discoverer of blood circulation, declared that all living things come from an egg: "ex ovo omnia." While that bold claim may appear to give women a high degree of agency in reproduction, Harvey instead vested breathtaking powers in male seed. Harvey used experiments to test traditional belief that, after intercourse, the uterus should contain a coagulated mass, fluid surrounded by a membrane, composed either of semen and menstrual blood (in Aristotle's theory) or male and female seed (Galen's theory). Harvey looked but could find no such thing, despite rounds of surgery on postcoital does whose uteri revealed no hint of it. This posed a problem. In Aristotle's terms the semen should be acting on the menstrual matter as a craftsman on raw material. But if male seed never touched the female stuff, then he had to imagine some other way whereby man's seed could work without direct contact. With some satisfaction at overturning antique theories, Harvey offered several metaphors for the seed's work. Perhaps the seed worked like a magnet, or like contagion, both of which caused effect from a distance. More ambitiously still, Harvey alleged the semen might work from afar like a thought or idea, simply from the strength of man's willing it, "from this Appetite or Conception is commeth to pass, that the female doth produce an offspring like the male Genitor." Harvey followed Aristotle comparing fertilization to man's conceiving a thought. Even more impressively, he proposed the seed could work by what we might call remote control, a willing into existence that Harvey likened to divine fiat, where the seed "doth operate with a vast discretion and providence . . . as if the Almighty himself should say, Let there be a production, and strait there is one." The woman's capacity was nowhere near as dazzling as the man's, even if everything did come from an egg.[19]

Those reproductive theorists confident that a woman had an egg were not sure what the egg was or how it might function. Was it, like a chicken's egg, nutrients for the embryo? Or did it contain something that helped make the embryo? Did it contain the new person in miniature whole? Was the egg always present in the woman's body or was it formed or expelled only during sex? German and Dutch scientists experimenting with microscopes in the next several decades came closer to finding the ovum, Niels Stensen (1638–1686) studying ovaries, and Regnier de Graaf (1641–1673) and Jan Swammerdam (1637–1680) finding what they supposed were eggs. As the mammalian egg was not seen until the nineteenth century and the human one not until the twentieth, researchers focused attention on the ovary, which, by mid-nineteenth century, some theorists treated as determinative of woman's whole being.[20]

## Conception and the Making of an Embryo

Theories of male and female anatomy carried implications for how the male caused a fetus in the female. What happened after male seed was delivered to a woman? The uterus was imagined as hungry for seed. The warmth and motion of sex might help the coagulating of the conceptus. The "heat of the womb fastens them," English midwife Jane Sharp wrote of embryos. The making of this ball of enclosed fluid needed action of the uterus, a heating or squeezing or clutching at the seed. In many accounts the seed was said to cause a kind of curdling or development of a crust, a shell, around a liquid mass. Hippocrates had intuited that this clotted blood mass would make the embryo. Aristotle argued that the male seed contains power that passes from the seed to the heart of the new embryo. Once that seed found a place, warmth, and matter, things got underway.[21]

Ongoing argument about the embryo focused less on the mechanics of its beginning than on its transformation from an undistinguished mass to a creature with distinct features. From ancient Greeks on, opinions favored schools of thought that either described the embryo's parts as preformed, needing simply to expand or unfold, or that described creatures' development through sequential stages. Aristotle detailed four stages, insistent that the rational soul appropriate to human beings could not be present until the matter was fit for it. This position, called delayed ensoulment or delayed hominization, assumes that the early embryo is not yet ready for a human soul. In Aristotle's progression, the embryo first had a nutritive soul (like plants), then a sensitive one (having touch, taste, sight, hearing), then a locomotive soul (like that of an animal with power of movement), and finally a rational soul. The conceptus changed stages as new-grown organs rendered it ready for that type of soul. Hippocrates and others were persuaded that boys developed much more rapidly than girls. Aristotle proposed that the male fetus was formed, attaining a human soul, around forty days, the female around ninety.[22]

Dante (1265–1321) attested to the persistence of this embryology. Statius in the Divine Comedy's *Purgatorio* explains that blood, perfect or concocted well from food, derives "effectual virtue, that informs [t]he several human limbs," and was emitted to a woman where it is "mingled with the other, one fitted to be passive and the other active." After this, the embryo proceeds through requisite stages:

[f]irst coagulating, then quickening that which
as its future matter, it has already thickened.

The active force, having now become a soul—
like a plant's but differing in this: it is still
on the way, while the plant has come to shore—

next functions, moving now and feeling,
like a sea-sponge, and from that goes on, producing
organs for the faculties of which it is the seed.

Now unfurls, now spreads the force, my son,
that comes straight from the heart of the begetter,
there where nature makes provision for all members. . . .

Open your heart to the truth that follows
and know that, once the brain's articulation
in the embryo arrives at its perfection,

the First Mover turns to it, rejoicing
in such handiwork of nature, and breathes
into it a spirit, new and full of power,

which then draws into its substance
all it there finds active and becomes a single soul
that lives, and feels, and reflects upon itself.[23]

Christian inheritors of Aristotle's theory of ensoulment made significant adjustments. Some church fathers considered that the soul might arise from within the embryo, Tertullian (160–220 CE) positing that it was given by the father from the beginning, Gregory of Nyssa (335–394 CE) suggesting that the soul initially was present but only became evident later. Augustine (354–430 CE) maintained at different times the soul's origin from within and outside of the fetus. Getting a soul into a creature that started as formless fluid was no simple thing. If the fetus required something from the father for ensoulment but only was slated to receive a human soul at forty days or so, it was not clear how that long-gone seed still could be providing the key element. The semen might linger a while, or it might transfer power to the fetal heart once that was formed. After the fifth century in western Europe, the view that God created the soul "specially and individually" grew increasingly prevalent. In the Middle Ages Thomas Aquinas furthered Aristotle's case for delayed ensoulment with modifications. For him, the embryo followed succession from plant-like stage to animal one to human soul, but with the intellectual soul infused by God at the last. This idea, that God added the soul directly to the formed fetus, kept many adherents into modernity, though more in the seventeenth century claimed immediate rather than delayed ensoulment.[24]

Understandably, parents and theorists alike had keen interest in discerning whether the developing embryo would turn out to be a girl or a boy. Some guessed sex had environmental causes, boys shaped on the right side of uterus, girls on the left. The mother's gaze resting on pictures of boys or even the word "boy" could help shape the correct sex. Whether through the prevailing of weaker seed or the truncating of full development, girls were thought to result from a process that went less well than hoped. Many took for granted that the boy "quickened" more quickly than the girl, in about half the time. With almost self-parodying consistency, premodern signs predicting the sex of a child toted up all the healthy, happy ones as proof of a coming boy and all the sallow sickliness as indicative of a girl. Nicholas Culpeper's (1616–1654) examples of sex predictors echo common bias: "The woman breeds a boy easier and with less pain than girls . . . the child is first felt by her on the right side; for the ancients are of the opinion that male children lie on the right side of the womb," and furthermore the "belly lies rounder and higher," the right breast is plumper and prominent, and the "color of a woman is more clear and not so swarthy as when she conceives a girl." The alternative was easily assessed: "contrary to these are signs of the conception of a female, and therefore it is needless to say anything of them."[25]

The embryo was thought to get to full-bodied stature either by staged development or by preexistence of parts. Preformation was one plausible solution to the puzzle of how a human-looking creature emerged from that initial shapeless bit. Instead of a theory of stages, the unfolding of already-formed parts made sense to Albrecht von Haller (1708–1777), who explained, "No part of the animal body is created after another and all are created and appear at the same time." Although theories akin to preformation existed among ancient philosophers, in the early modern period technology enabled a clearer view of the embryo. Preformationists contended in several directions, against those who prioritized fertilization or insisted on stages of development, and also among themselves, between those who thought the key component for humans came from the father or the mother. Some preformationists maintained that each embryo was folded up inside its parent beforehand, potentially all embryos prepackaged all the way back to Adam and Eve. Those who thought the whole fetus was in the egg were "ovists" and those who found all in spermatozoa were "spermists" or "animalculists." Either position, putting all in sperm or all in egg, rendered the other parent nearly irrelevant. Preformation as a plausible theory was defeated by eighteenth-century experiments demonstrating the necessity of fertilization.[26]

Much productive research on embryos in eighteenth- and nineteenth-century Europe advanced nearer to current understanding. Comparing reproductive processes and embryos from other animals—worms, chicken, fish, and amphibians—was especially useful. Researchers demonstrated that early embryos of varied species started with similar parts and that complex structures emerged from visibly simpler ones. Given the landscape of nineteenth-century science, debates about embryos fell squarely into controversy regarding the origin of species, embryologists taking up questions made unavoidable by evolution. Perhaps most famous in these debates is Ernst Haeckel (1834–1919), whose theory that "ontogeny replicates phylogeny" was supported by not-quite-accurate sketches of salamander, pig, rabbit, and other embryos alongside human ones. Arguing that the development of the individual embryo repeats the evolution of species, Haeckel's famous illustrations show the resemblance of early humans to putatively lower animals. Such illustrations insisted that the human most certainly does not start as a fully formed little man but in early stages looks very much like an embryonic fish or dog, with gill slits and tail.[27]

Within these arguments about how a baby comes to be, woman's deeds are conspicuously absent. Her body may or may not be offering seed or stuff for the making of a baby, her ungovernable uterus may or may not be greedily grabbing at what a man had sown inside—either way, there was not that much she could or should do about it. Passive did not mean inert. Occasionally writers gave some credit to gestation. Stumbling over punctuation so as not to slight the male's elevated function, *The Birth of Mankind* (1540) allowed, "although that man may be as principal mover in the cause of generation, yet (no displeasure to men), the woman doth confer and contribute much more." To be sure, what the writer credited to women, beyond being "receptacle," was nourishment before and *after* birth. From descriptions of fertilization contrasting immobile ovum to speedy sperm, to accounts of birth attributing action to the baby, women were cast in roles passive rather than active. The *making* part of making a baby was not attributed to the mother, even though theorists across millennia accounted differently for this passivity. Preformation and epigenesis both made gestation nearly irrelevant. Thus what some guide-writers called "directions for breeding women" should be approached in terms of this presumed passivity.[28]

This passivity underscores a sharp irony. The long-ago woman was thought to have little power to *make* a baby but she was ascribed considerable power to damage the one a man generated in her. Therefore the relatively minimal prenatal care instruction offered to pregnant women in guides before the nineteenth century addressed two priorities. She should avoid causing harm and try to maintain her own health. Following a few rules would help keep her from wrecking what the man had wrought. The rules also aimed to improve women's comfort while waiting out this condition. Mostly the short instructional chapters in these guides resemble advice now given to airline travelers encountering turbulence: sit back and do whatever you can to make yourself relatively comfortable until this journey, over whose results you have almost no control, has come to an end.

### Directions for Breeding Women

Surveying midwives' manuals from the sixteenth and seventeenth centuries, Merry Wiesner-Hanks remarks that these guides kept reprinting much of the same material and "their advice for expectant mothers changed little," indeed, that "[m]uch of what they advise is still recommended today." She is correct that modest diet, wardrobe, and exercise are counseled then and now, but in significant respects the old advice is quite far from ours. The most conspicuous difference between older and newer advice for pregnant women is the extent of it. Two widely circulating English books in the early modern period, Nicholas Culpeper's *Directory for Midwives* and *Aristotle's Masterpiece*, give brief "Directions for Breeding Women." These "Directions" come in a short chapter wedged between one on untimely births and tips on discovering a baby's sex. Its location and brevity are intentional, bits of advice to help the woman avoid making the baby come out too early. In his 1699 text, *A Companion for Midwives*, Robert Barret made duties and dangers similarly explicit, titling his prenatal advice "what Conduct she ought to observe during the Time of her being with Child, so as to prevent Miscarriage." Women's digestion most worried writers. When "breeding," women were told they should only drink moderate amounts of wine and should not exercise or dance too much, so that they would not suffocate, starve, or expel the child. They should also try to control what they thought and saw.[29]

Some guides urged the woman to watch the body for signs of conception because success of a pregnancy depended on her not interrupting it. Guidebooks well into the twentieth century listed the signs that should make a woman suspect pregnancy—missed period, frequent urination, breast tenderness, nausea, and eventually fetal movement—but declared that this imperfect assurance was enough. As we do, premoderns tried to tease the secret out of urine but their methods of "uromancy," like using urine to sprout barley or to make rusty spots on needles, remained unreliable. The only certain confirmation came when the mother felt the fetus move. Fetal movement, "quickening," was taken as hard proof of a woman's pregnancy, evidence of the baby's ensouled presence. Still, some guidebooks laid heavy burdens on women not to mistake pregnancy for some kind of menstrual blockage. "Ignorance makes women to be murderers to the fruit of their owne bodies," writers thundered.[30]

Such advice illustrates the passive-but-perilous capacity assumed of pregnant women. Just do no harm was the substance of "directions for breeding women." Beyond inadvertently causing miscarriage, women were feared capable of many other injuries through their eyes, brain, limbs, and even generative parts. Aversion to sex was sometimes counted a symptom of likely pregnancy ("her desire to *Venus* is abated"), which was useful since the pregnant woman was told to "abstain from Venery in the first months." Intercourse could endanger the work of the womb or cause "superfetation," conception of an additional fetus after the first one was underway. It may seem implausible to imagine that children could be stained or wounded by a pregnant woman's mundane doings. But such beliefs arose from understandable sources, fear of causing birth defects, and from perceived helplessness in either discerning their causes or preventing them.[31]

## Maternal Impressions and "Monsters"

Stuart Blakely, an obstetrician in upstate New York in the early twentieth century, was unfazed by the startling superstitions he heard from his childbearing patients, reasoning that "[t]he remarkable processes, dangers, and results of these periods of a woman's life must have been a profound mystery and source of wonder to the untutored mind of savage man." In past centuries, and even now to some extent, doctors and patients sometimes have no accurate way to explain what causes one fetus to develop differently when hundreds of others fare well. Doctors now might discover a chromosomal disorder but cannot do anything about it; they can recognize a rare condition but not explain how or why it appeared in that particular child. Antique worry over a pregnant woman's thoughts and deeds at base aimed to discover why births went wrong. The answers were, and still are, hard to find. Until medicine can diagnose, explain, and prevent all such occurrences, expectant parents are not unreasonable to fish around for answers handed down to them by forbears. Thus Blakely, in an age when medicine felt itself forward-looking and fearless in dispelling ignorance, was unsurprised to hear among his patients, "if one but ask and listen, so many echoes of the race's dim and pagan past, down the long road of woman's memory."[32]

Judging from the sheer volume of antique warnings about it, the mother's mind was thought to possess more fearsome power to harm than her body. Efforts to explain birth defects fell under the head-ing of teratology, sometimes described as the study of "monsters" or "prodigies," terms that in old usage could count anything from slight impediments to anencephaly to molar pregnancies. Some births were described sensationally, exaggerating the strangeness of a baby's shape or striving to compare fetal attributes to those of beasts. Theorists gravitated to a few possibilities. Some thought defects could spring from problems with seed, others blamed the position of the stars or alignment of the cosmos during gestation, and others centered on the strength of the mothers' "impressions." Belief in maternal impressions has a certain logic. It was far from obvious to the naked eye—then and now—how the conceptus turned into a child. One weakness with a reproductive theory assuming male seed made children was explaining how things went wrong. If seed came from both men and women, perhaps the weaker one prevailed or something went awry in the blending. If the problem were not the fault of the seed, it likelier could be the fault of the woman. This conclusion was the corollary of the male seed's potency, as Thomas Laqueur explains, "Since normal conception is, in a sense, the male having an idea in the female's body, then abnormal conception, the mola, is a conceit for her having an ill-gotten and inadequate idea of her own."[33]

Maternal impressions were the means by which women were presumed to do most harm to the growing fetus. A complex group of notions with ancient pedigree, maternal impressions named belief that the mother somehow touched the developing body of the fetus through her mind, through fear, imagination, thought, or desire. Women's ideas during pregnancy could mark a baby or ruin the pregnancy altogether. Once born, the baby could be seen as a sort of transcript recording the worries, cravings, or fantasies that had been harbored by the woman during gestation. Students of teratology gathered examples curated to shock: the child whose face appeared froglike because his mother held a frog shortly before going to bed with her husband; the child born with maimed feet because his mother wore too-tight shoes; and, perhaps most notoriously ludicrous, an example from the seventeenth century of "the child with a mussel for a head, who nevertheless lived for eleven years, receiving liquid nourishment from a spoon into the gaping bivalve; of course the mother had longed for sea-mussels in her pregnancy."[34]

Absurd though the mussel-head example is, it at least touches a principle confirmed by later research, that food can shape fetal development. Not only could food be influential, but its connection with the woman's mind and emotions, fueling inordinate desire, could be dangerous. Sometimes this guilt was charged to pregnant women themselves; in other accounts, women were thought victims of the desire, required to obey it, as in the fairy tale of Rapunzel. Rapunzel's poor mother needed to eat the herb lest she die, so her husband stole it and was caught, both parents forced to offer up the child of her belly for the sake of its craving. Other worries about fetal marking target not food cravings but a woman's inappropriate sexual ones. An adulterous woman whose thoughts strayed to her lover during pregnancy (or, worse, during conception) could give her child that other man's appearance or, conversely, could inscribe her husband's looks on illegitimate offspring if she thought hard on it.

Thinking about things, especially things deemed inappropriate for female minds, could stain the baby. Pregnant women appeared vulnerable to shocks and fears. Frightening or hairy or injured animals could cause a woman to birth a child unusually colored, unusually hairy, or lacking fingers, toes, arms, or legs. Though the mechanism of this marking remained elusive—some thought it came from a kind of sympathy between woman and fetus—the idea persisted into the nineteenth century even among the educated. With access to new anatomical knowledge and, later, to microscopes, seventeenth- and eighteenth-century researchers debated its validity rather than assuming it as fact. British medical writers Daniel Turner and James Blondel conducted a vituperative exchange early in the eighteenth century, the latter rejecting maternal impressions. Widespread belief in them kept on, if under challenge, in the 1726 scandal of English servant Mary Toft who claimed, after being startled by a rabbit in a field and craving rabbit meat, to give birth to a litter of bunnies. Toft was believed by some doctors and came to royal attention, though she was found to be propagating only falsehood.[35]

While maternal impressions tried to explain a range of pregnancy symptoms and birth conditions, teratology was the chief concern. If a child were born with a face like a frog, and neither mother nor father looked like a frog, the woman's behavior could help trace what happened. When the likeliest alternative explanation credited alignment of the planets, maternal impressions offered reasonable causal connection. Paradoxically, the theory of maternal impressions paid ambivalent respect to women's contribution to the work of making the baby. Maternal impressions counted women able to influence the fetus, though this influence was out of their control.[36]

Power to do much and interesting harm hardly redounds to the praise of the childbearing woman, maternal impressions a belief making mothers-to-be resemble Disney's horned witch Maleficent, bane of Sleeping Beauty, uninvited to the blessing of the babe but potent yet to curse. As professional medicine in the United States concluded over a century ago, maternal impressions are mythical. Most American doctors even from the late nineteenth century denounced the notion as an old wives' tale. Doctors' vehement disapproval of maternal impressions sprang from the same misunderstanding that fueled the notion in the first place, that women had very little to do with successful births, that the baby generated by the father could plug along well enough on his own.

### Lying-In with Midwives and Gossips

The premodern mother who successfully avoided all these pitfalls finally would find herself at term and ready to be delivered of the baby. Ready, but when? Tradition held that a baby could be born healthily at seven months or at nine, but not eight. Culpeper, naming a seventh- or ninth-month birth "legitimate," deemed an "illegitimate birth" one that came at the wrong time, at eighth month or too late, though he claimed that successful gestations had lasted as long as fourteen or fifteen months. Astrology provided another explanation for the eight-month-old's sad fate, *Aristotle's Masterpiece* clarifying this theory: since "in the eighth month Saturn doth predominate, which is cold and dry; and coldness being an utter enemy to life, destroyes the nature of the child." Old accounts of childbirth itself also underscored maternal passivity. Analyzing Harvey's reproductive ideas about hens and humans, Eve Keller observes that for Harvey, "[e]ven the act of birth is a wholly passive process for the mother, since the fetus, both fowl and human, releases itself from its place of growth." Birth-advice writers thought the fetus would move out when the space became too cramped or food was subpar, fighting to be freed from imprisonment in the mother. The fetus, not the mother, was supposed the active party making an exit.[37]

When the fetus got ready to exit, it was time to call the midwife. Their occupational title meaning "with woman," midwives helped with births in the ancient world, disobeying Pharaoh and rescuing Moses, and have been purported among the first witnesses of the birth of Jesus.[38] A range of other persons may have assisted births in periods of scarcer records through the early Middle Ages: neighbors, relatives, husbands. Midwifery resurged by the thirteenth century in Europe. To preserve modesty and make useful their own experience as women, midwives were favored attendants for helping women through childbirth. Their training often was practical rather than formal, midwives learning by assisting at births. Midwives have been regulated by civil and ecclesiastical authorities, occupying an office to uphold public goods and attest to misdeeds like illegitimacy or adultery or infanticide. In households with adequate space and assistance to permit it, childbirth in early modern Europe occurred in a lying-in chamber, bringing the midwife to the birthing woman's home. Lying-in included labor and recovery for weeks after birth. Often other women, "god-sibs" or "gossips" would gather to assist. Sequestered in a space closed or curtained off for privacy, isolated even to the sealing of keyholes, the midwife and helpers prepared linens, offered food, drink, or remedies, kept the birthing woman company, and offered comfort.[39]

Birthing done lying down on the back in bed is of relatively recent vintage. The birthing stool, a chair with an open seat, was preferred for this hard work. Sometimes mothers were advised to hold their breath so the "guts and entrails be thrust together and depressed downward," helping the baby's egress. Midwives not only provided presence but expertise in minimizing pain, finding suitable positions, and addressing difficulties birth could present. The importance of baptism in Roman Catholic doctrine suited midwives to perform emergency baptism, lest the baby die without benefit of the sacrament. In Catholic understanding, baptism is necessary for salvation, so it was better to have this office performed irregularly at delivery than not at all. Furthermore, a fetus that could not be brought out alive still would have to be brought out. Not until the sixteenth century were cesarean sections at all likely to yield a living woman and child. After successful birth, the newly delivered woman would spend several weeks resting to complete her confinement.[40]

Midwives before the modern period sometimes came into conflict with male doctors, but generally were not perceived as competing for work that belonged to men. They provided a service appropriate for their sex. Physicians might consult or a barber-surgeon might be called in to extract an obstructed delivery. The absence of physicians from the birthing bed reflected both the state of premodern medicine and the manners of birth. They could not insure survival much more reliably than herbalist, lay healer, or midwife. Some midwives were better than others, but their fitness to practice their work was widely granted. Beyond exceptional cases, men stayed mostly out of birthing chambers until several developments drew them in. Sixteenth- and seventeenth-century studies of anatomy and physiology raised the value of knowledge and more systematic training, only available to men. The French were leaders in developing new approaches to birth, improving methods in charity maternity hospitals in Paris. Male practitioners introduced tools to assist births. The invention of forceps offers a bitter example of conflict over instruments. Devised by Peter Chamberlen (1560–1631), of a Huguenot medical family living in England, the instrument was composed of two hinged spoons that would allow the birth attendant to ease out a fetus more effectively than by hand or—lethally—by hook. This obstetric advancement served the family's theatricality and desire for profit: the Chamberlens were called to bedside of a delivery in crisis, bringing the lifesaving instrument concealed in a chest, expelling others from the room so as not to give away the secret. By the early eighteenth century other physicians were using versions of forceps. Many midwives remained wary, insisting that their experience and skill was better for women than men's brutal tools.[41]

Man-midwives, or accoucheurs, became fashionable in the seventeenth century and beyond, serving at some royal and noble births and inspiring other women to try their services too. Midwives and doctors collaborated in some cases. In other instances, man-midwifery and obstetrics rose through active suppression of female practitioners. As man-midwives multiplied, female practitioners fought back with defenses of their skill. In London in the 1740s, enterprising man-midwife William Smellie (1697–1763) sought to establish training programs for other men, a plan opposed by midwives. Smellie and his allies contended in print with midwife Elizabeth Nihell (1723–1776), an accomplished woman who had trained in Paris and articulated a positive case for the care of women by women. Still, male presence at childbed grew.[42]

Midwives may have had little formal training in much of early modern Europe and later in colonial and nineteenth-century America, but many guides were written to assist them. After all, men kept keen interest in writing about what they called "the secrets of women." Eucharius Rösslin's 1513 *Rosegarden,* one of only three guides directed immediately to midwives published in nearly a thousand years, was translated and reprinted many times.[43] It was amended in English several decades later by Richard Jonas and Thomas Reynalde as *The Birth of Mankind.* Swiss physician Jacob Rueff (1500–1558) published *De Conceptu e Generatione Hominis* in 1554, later translated as *The Ex-*

*pert Midwife.* France provided uncommonly extensive training of birth attendants through maternity hospitals in Paris and supported the efforts of some women to improve the work of their colleagues. Louise Bourgeois (1563–1636), court midwife to the household of Henry IV of France, wrote a casebook to instruct others. Angelique Marguerite le Boursier du Coudray (1712–1794) received commission from Louis XV to travel across France for training and inspection of midwives. Silesian midwife Justine Siegemund (1636–1705) wrote a catechism describing birth techniques. Jane Sharp (ca. 1641–ca. 1671) is reputed to be the first woman to publish an English-language guide. Other guides flowed forth in the seventeenth and eighteenth centuries, sometimes addressing primarily midwives, otherwise coaching literate women in describing symptoms to caregivers.[44]

### It Is Not the Sick Who Need a Doctor but the Healthy

The shift from midwife- to doctor-attended births was replayed in the United States. Midwives predominated in the colonial period, sometimes collaborating with frontier doctors. As in Europe, hiring a doctor was usual in emergencies and grew more fashionable for middle- and upper-class women in normal births. Midwives and doctors operated somewhat differently in Southern states, where slaveholders had compelling interest in the delivery of offspring, especially offspring who became their property. Slave women occupy a critical, bitter place in the history of American obstetrics, both by their use as subjects for research and from their expertise in midwifery. James Marion Sims, controversial pioneer of techniques in gynecology, did surgical experiments on slave women without consent or anesthesia. White women within plantation households trusted enslaved midwives to attend their births, often favoring them over male physicians.[45]

Births by midwife dropped through the nineteenth and twentieth centuries. Some historians of American childbirth emphasize that this change followed women's choices. Women increasingly chose births overseen by male practitioners, though often at home until nearly the mid-twentieth century. While midwifery's decline in part followed choices made by birthing women, the elevation of obstetrics was accomplished at the expense of midwifery. Raising the status of their profession required obstetricians to distinguish themselves from general practitioners, to demonstrate that they really had sophisticated knowledge and technique—and also to disadvantage midwives by means of law, propaganda, and obstructed access to institutions. Though some doctors supported trained midwives, others played on stereotypes of midwives as dirty, ignorant, and primitive, recommending abolition of the craft. Midwives held out longer in southern states and in northern cities with immigrant populations. Prominent Chicago obstetrician Joseph DeLee spoke for more than a few in his profession when he characterized midwives as "a drag on our progress as a science and art, a *relic of barbarism.*"[46]

Two game-changing developments transformed birth by the mid-twentieth century. Better living came through chemistry: it became possible to give birth without pain and with much less chance of dying in the process. The first of these breakthroughs came in the 1840s. In the Boston area, Harvard midwifery professor Walter Channing championed the use of ether in deliveries. Women unconscious through the worst parts of birth could experience it as painless. Meanwhile, around the same time, Scottish physician James Young Simpson perfected use of chloroform, whose popularity soared when Queen Victoria took it gladly during a delivery in 1853. Controversial, easy to overdose, and blamed for reversing Eve's curse, the drugs made women unconscious during delivery. Though these drugs had defenders and detractors on both sides of the Atlantic, they were received warmly by well-heeled Victorian women for whom they removed the agony of childbirth—an agony exacerbated by period costumes favoring narrow waists, requiring corsets that disordered reproductive organs.[47]

Well-heeled women also made fashionable a technique that followed in the early twentieth century. Twilight sleep, *Dämmerschlaf*, originated in Freiburg, Germany, and came to the United States in the second decade of the twentieth century. In it patients remained conscious and could feel pain, thrashing and crying out so that they were restrained with straitjackets while under the influence. Because the drugs blotted out this memory, twilight-sleep patients happily would awaken with no memory of the hardship of birth. The fad was short-lived, with resistance from some doctors and the death of one of its chief boosters crushing its popularity. Twentieth-century American women continued to receive more options for less pain, by oral, rectal, or spinal channels. Baby-boom birthrates made efficiency a virtue, so that general anesthesia grew common for delivery until later in the century. In the late 1950s, Johns Hopkins obstetrician Nicholson Eastman boasted, "even that old bugbear of childbirth, the pain of labor, has been so assuaged that the majority of American mothers today are unconscious of the actual birth of the baby." Natural-birth advocacy from the 1950s on, plus concerns about fetal effects, nudged general anesthesia out of favor, though spinal blocks and epidurals thereafter enabled conscious birth minus pain.[48]

Even more revolutionary for safe births was discovery of antiseptics to kill germs during delivery and antibiotics to counter infections from the process. The use of chemicals like chlorine to kill germs entered medical practice with controversy. Urged to wash and disinfect hands and instruments, some doctors resisted allegations that *they* could be the cause of their maternity patients' death, redistributing something evil on their hands or coats or hair as they moved from cadaver to laboring woman. Puerperal fever was a threat especially in maternity hospitals, likelier to be spread there than when patients birthed at home. Antibiotics, wonder drugs made available in the 1930s and 1940s, could be administered to women with signs of puerperal fever and dramatically pull mother and child back from brink of death.[49]

These additions to the birth process drew it more thoroughly into the sphere of medical management. Wanting a painless birth and wanting drugs that could save a life encouraged women to view birth as necessitating medical intervention. During World War II, many women previously outside the orbit of hospital childbirth accessed it through the US government–funded Emergency Maternity and Infant Care (EMIC) program. From 1943 to 1949 the EMIC provided pre- and postnatal care to families of servicemen, paying for one of seven US births and managing over a million and a half maternity cases. For a mid-twentieth-century American woman, hospital birth had a lot to recommend it. Even when doctors were brusque and labor was processed in assembly-line fashion, hospital protocols offered release from the pain of birth and, not inconsiderably, a quieter way to recover than being in the midst of housekeeping and family demands. It appeared modern and desirable.[50]

A consequence, partly designed, of the shift to doctor-hospital birth was the rise of prenatal care as a way of defining the experience of pregnancy. The logic of doctors' care over the whole course of gestation, it could be argued, was implicit even in early midwifery manuals.

Prenatal care extended doctors' dominion over the whole duration. It developed in late nineteenth- and early twentieth-century medical communities, especially in Britain and the United States, from the logic that monitoring a few dangerous conditions before birth could greatly increase maternal-fetal health at birth. Complications could arise from syphilis, diabetes, and other maternal maladies. By regularly checking a woman in advance, doctors could avoid tragedy.[51]

Not just sick women would go to doctors but healthy ones. Indeed, that curious reversal was at the heart of this new deal. The healthy pregnancy depended on the woman becoming a patient. Promoted by leading obstetricians like J. Whitridge Williams in the United States and John William Ballantyne in Britain (where it is called antenatal care), this preventative approach advanced a number of aims at once: improving maternal-infant health, providing opportunity for research, and raising the reputation of obstetrics. Williams's successor, Nicholson Eastman, opens his maternity manual by assuring women that "pregnancy should be a healthy, happy time. But health and happiness in pregnancy are dependent in large measure upon proper guidance by a competent physician." Coinciding and sometimes clashing with enthusiasm over eugenics, this approach contended that women's good "hygiene" could affect birth outcomes powerfully, if not as much as heredity. If an infant were well begotten but ill borne, Ballantyne remarks, he "may be no less a derelict than the child of many generations of a morbid heredity." Concern over environmental impacts on public health led doctors and policy makers to help babies by improving women's health since, in Ballantyne's words, the "mother is the unborn infant's immediate environment . . . in her, if we may use a phrase used more often with a higher sphere of things, he lives and moves and has his being."[52]

Prenatal care evolved from a targeted approach for at-risk women to a comprehensive one for all pregnant women. Realization that the maternal environment could affect the baby generated new "commandments in hygiene" that the mother "must obey." As Ballantyne's urgent language suggests, new understandings of fetal development justified new pressure on women. In a metaphor his early modern antecedents would have appreciated, Ballantyne compares baby-making to pottery. The potter may start with perfectly good clay and end up with a bad product because of error in the handling, drying, firing, glazing, whereas "the expert workman may do much even with an inferior material, whilst in the hands of the bungler the finest substance may be fatally spoiled." As pregnancy became increasingly likely to end with doctor at the foot of a hospital bed, prenatal care became the preferred path to that endpoint. Indeed, it became the defining framework of the whole experience. Whereas childbearing had been an intimate topic, discussed by women but with "virtual silence surrounding pregnancy" in public, doctors helped make it acceptable to discuss in polite company.[53]

And this is approximately where we still are. Three milestones conventionally get grouped together on history-of-reproduction timelines to draw that story near to our present. Discovery of the mammalian ovum came only in 1827, when Karl Ernst von Baer published a paper telling of it. That milestone should astonish, a reminder that until then science could not confirm even the existence of a female counterpart to the male "seed." In 1876 Haeckel's student Wilhelm Oscar Hertwig observed sea urchin fertilization as a fusion of cells, refuting preformation. In the United States, Edgar Allen sighted the human ovum in 1928. Noteworthy about the discovery of female contributions to reproduction not only is how late the news came, but how little change in assumption it wrought. Until these pieces were in place Americans could not know the story we now hold to be self-evident. There was no sperm-meets-egg-makes-baby story to explain the newborn until that time. Understanding genetics and endocrinology took another few decades. If the origin of a baby long had been assumed an achievement of man, woman's contribution uncertain and inferior, discoveries that she contributed half might have been revolutionary. They were not. Recognition that women not only gave their half but also shaped genetic stuff and fetal development through prenatal actions might have drawn dazzlement, sure, but they also might have inspired reflection about the nature of prenatal work. If what was actually true about gestation turned out to be totally different from what was long assumed, some big thinking was in order, even a new culture of birth.

In the centuries before ours people asked questions about childbearing that connected the experience more closely to its explanation. They asked what men and women gave to make a baby, how bodies brought forth a new soul, how the process happened to women. They used tools at their disposal to come up with meaningful answers. We ask some of the same questions but, so charmed by our powerful tools, sometimes stop short of answers. We substitute the tools for the answers. To get to more adequate answers, we could use some of these tools in new ways. Premodern people did not use the insights of theology as well as they might to understand pregnancy, but we can. Premodern people did not evaluate well the work of pregnancy because they thought it was passive, but we can. Premodern people did not have the luxury to do much navel gazing because they had no fetal image, no knowledge of what was developing day by day, but did have awareness of the likelihood of mother's mortality. We have fewer babies per woman with more consciousness about it, but shy away from reflecting on it too much.

Instead, with doctors dismissing old approaches as foolish and unsanitary, medicine did not so much substitute a new culture for the old superstitions as appear to remove childbearing from culture. New manners or customs developing around pregnancy were mediated by medicine. An ideal metaphor for what happened to childbearing may be unavailable. But we might compare it to health professionals, say, abolishing Thanksgiving dinner, offering protein shakes and supplement tablets in its stead as safer and healthier. That approach probably *would* be safer and healthier. Traditional American Thanksgiving gets plenty wrong about both menu and history. Of course, the traditional holiday comes entangled with personal sentiment and custom and civic observance, so a healthy substitute might be able to provide nutrition but none of the rest. Humans, being what they are, might try to rebuild customs around the new healthy Thanksgiving, arranging a smoothie bowl in Aunt Mary's casserole dish or spilling vitamins from a cornucopia, but these garnishes would appear quaint or ridiculous.

We have traded assumption of mother's passivity for a strenuous program of prenatal duties. We have traded an officially approved biology that assumed men did everything for one recognizing women contribute more than half. But the customs, manners, and reflections around pregnancy never really recovered from the paradigm shift. For this reason, observing changing views of pregnancy through prenatal care manuals opens opportunity to think differently about it. We can begin to consider afresh what kind of work this is, now that we know it is active and not passive. We can consider how the biology of pregnancy reflects the connectedness and generosity of human life.

## A Book for Every Woman

When novelist Leo Tolstoy discovered a winsome volume by Alice Bunker Stockham (1833–1912), he liked it so much that he wrote a preface for the Russian translation and declared it a book "every thoughtful woman" should read. Stockham, one of the yet-rare female physicians in late nineteenth-century America, approached self-care during pregnancy as a gift to future generations. The book Tolstoy admired was her 1880s pregnancy guide titled, *Tokology: A Book for Every Woman.* It taught women how to care for the pregnant body. Stockham's subtitle highlights a fundamental assumption of a new generation of pregnancy manuals. These books began to presume both that women needed this advice and that a book was the appropriate source of it. Of course similar writing had existed before. But the batch of maternity writing arising after the late nineteenth century reflects the expectation that every pregnant woman should read a book, and that reading a book was becoming an essential part of the experience.[54]

These books privatized the act of seeking advice on pregnancy to some degree, the woman checking a silent page rather than talking to friend or relative to get an answer, but they also enabled a new public manner of talking about pregnancy. Marika Seigel, studying rhetorical strategies of how-to books for expectant mothers, notes that "mainstream" pregnancy manuals (like *What to Expect When You're Expecting* or *Pregnancy for Dummies* in our own time) serve as a sort of orientation to the rules of prenatal care, teaching women to interpret their personal condition in terms of a shared narrative about what pregnancy is supposed to be. Women learn to "know" themselves in terms of this shared story about how pregnancy works. Early manuals took pains to justify themselves, to explain to women (and sometimes to fathers-to-be) why books were needed to help get a healthy baby.[55]

In our own time we take our need for this information so much for granted that we no longer have to be talked into taking it. American women tend to take popularized versions of obstetrics (OB) office advice as essential, personalizing the process through small acts of disobedience (a glass of wine!), but otherwise to be taken as prescribed. To stretch the Thanksgiving metaphor a bit, it is like coming to think of Thanksgiving as the holiday where everyone stuffs themselves with protein shakes. We take the prenatal care culture of pregnancy so much for granted that we forget it *is* a kind of culture—behaving as though this OB-visit-trimester-countdown is what pregnancy just is. This is why study of the prenatal care manuals featured below is valuable. As relatively early entries in the genre, they remain self-aware enough to recognize the prenatal care program as formative of a new set of manners and expectations, and to reveal remnants here and there of what that new set was replacing.

A book for every woman: as in our own time, these earlier prenatal manuals sought to be different things for different readers. This book cannot examine all the prenatal manuals that ever have circulated in English, but focuses on a few chosen as representative and influential, though others also get briefer mention. A brief introduction of the principals may be helpful.

Stockham's book and Prudence Saur's *Maternity: A Book for Every Wife and Mother* fit a group of American guides blending new counsels of prenatal care with old-fashioned sentiment. Books by physician S. Josephine Baker (1873–1945) and nurse Carolyn Van Blarcom (1875–1961) bear some similarities. Their basic instructions are offered along with a kind of apology telling readers why they would want the book.

From across the Atlantic, *Expectant Motherhood* by Dr. J. W. Ballantyne (1861–1923) is an influential guide translating medical advice for the interested female reader. The maternity reforms of John Shields Fairbairn (1865–1944), another British obstetrician, inspired the prenatal care manuals of his students Minnie Randell and Cyril V. Pink (1894–1965). Randell, lead nurse among maternity patients at St. Thomas's Hospital in London, offered *Training for Childbirth from the Mother's Point of View* and the physician Pink, an advocate of vegetarianism, gave *The Foundations of Motherhood*.[56]

Guides appearing nearer to the middle of the twentieth century display the genre at ease with itself. Nicholson J. Eastman (1895–1973) wrote the oft-reprinted *Expectant Motherhood. The Catholic Guide to Expectant Motherhood*, authored by three doctors and a priest, takes the now-familiar guide structure and adds religious distinctives, like choice of godparents and natural spacing of children. A very different idiom repackages familiar content in *Modeling for Motherhood* by Doris Hale Heinz and Katherine Smith Bolt, a girlfriends' guide written not in nurse's language but with a chatty, irreverent lilt.[57]

Finally, a remarkable set of guides that offers a long view of the culture of pregnancy in the United States has the distinction of being produced by the US government. The Children's Bureau, a Progressive-era institution situated variously in Labor, Social Security, and Health departments across its tenure, published research and instructional materials on child health, education, poverty, and working conditions. From 1913 to 1983 the bureau published millions of copies of *Prenatal Care*, a booklet that through its revisions over time illustrates big changes in expectations of pregnancy. The guide shows the transition of pregnancy into a "way of life." These guides, even where their insights fumble, supply equipment for evaluating childbearing as appreciable work.[58]

# 3

## *Acting and Showing*

[T]he mother herself... must be taught she is an active agent, not a passive sufferer. She must regard herself as an athlete in need of training for her special job, not a poor invalid who must lie down and have the sympathy and prayers of all lest she die of it.

—Kathleen O. Vaughan, *Safe Childbirth* (1937)

Communal existence is not a predicament, a second-best option or necessary evil, and the way new members of the race are brought forth—their initial dependency on their parents—serves to illuminate that truth very clearly.... the secret to the meaning of human life—our need of each other—is given away by its newest members.

—James Mumford, *Ethics at the Beginning of Life* (2013)

W hat is a pregnant woman actually doing? Something or nothing? Retiring the old view that pregnancy is mostly passive
leaves space to consider what kind of act it is. We should make good use
of that space. While faulty science, higher birthrates, and higher infant
mortality may have thrown up obstacles to lofty reflection on pregnancy even among those in the past equipped to reflect well, current
conditions may make it more possible to see rightly what always has
been at play. Old models of reproduction are set aside. The timing and
success of pregnancies can be anticipated better and in some measure
controlled. Those conditions give opportunity to consider this chapter's opening question—what is going on here?—rather than sapping
popular interest because doctors have things under control.

Prenatal instruction guides sketch the outlines of that work, medical personnel fill in the details, pregnant women are supposed to follow
orders, and bystanders hold them accountable. More accurate views
of how reproduction happens not only highlight the involuntary functions that sustain childbearing but highlight ways that women facilitate
the process. Carrying a baby in utero is active, a kind of awareness and
a kind of work. Being present to that development, recognizing the
occurrence for what it is and allowing its display through the body,
constitutes the witness of pregnancy. Those elements, what a woman
does and what a woman shows, give this intimate condition a public
dimension.

A pregnant woman obviously is doing *something*. We know sex has
something to do with the subsequent arrival of a baby, but sex by itself
does not accomplish the baby. Unlike a nineteenth-century woman,
writing to her husband, who reported, "all I can do, is to wait patiently,"
we no longer assume that all a pregnant woman can do is wait and pray.[1]
The woman's body grows and changes shape. She does many things

that she would not ordinarily do. After some months a baby appears. It seems plausible to conclude that the woman did something beyond the initial act to *make* the baby, or at least to help growth along. Even now, residual assumptions that the mother is basically passive persist, right alongside urgent warnings for her to do many things to get a healthy baby. The link between her deeds and the baby's health remains fuzzy even as prenatal commands grow more arduous.

Prenatal vitamins offer a good example of this contradiction. American women who avail themselves of medical care in pregnancy might receive a prescription for special vitamins at a first OB visit, or even before. Starting to take these vitamins is a gesture of cultural significance, one of the acts through which a woman acknowledges she is pregnant. Similar vitamin varieties are available over the counter, but OB patients often are offered special ones available only by prescription. These may or may not be more expensive than vitamins on the shelf but are distinguished by being recommended, even mandated, by the woman's doctor. What makes them different from ordinary multivitamins mostly is a higher concentration of iron, calcium, and folic acid. The first two a pregnant woman needs in greater amounts than usual because she will produce more blood and the fetus requires building material for bones. Folic acid, the synthetic form of the B vitamin folate, is a special case. When, in the latter decades of the twentieth century, researchers correlated deficiencies of folate with resultant neural tube defects, this vitamin took on the character of a nearly miraculous substance. Folic acid became a sort of magic pill, what pregnant women could take and thereby stave off neural tube defects like spina bifida or anencephaly.[2]

Discovering the need for folate early in pregnancy fortified prenatal care as a shaper of the experience of pregnancy. Requiring this vitamin magnified the authority of the doctor over pregnancy and, consequently, the urgency of following a doctor's orders. Doctors showed that their guild knew something important about childbearing that the public at large could not figure out on its own, and lack of knowledge could bring enormous harm. Since an ordinary woman cannot be expected to, say, eat enough folate-rich foods to rescue her baby from potential problems unless the doctor tells her to do it, taking prenatal vitamins signals her need of that instruction. This clear connection between expertise and prevention of harm makes women take up the prenatal vitamins, but it also encourages willingness to follow doctors' orders on additional directives as well. If doctors know best about folic acid, they probably know best about everything else too. To be sure, a woman could simply purchase separate doses of vitamins and take them as desired. But the acts of receiving a prescription from the doctor, purchasing from a pharmacy the necessary pills, and taking them faithfully each day, represent a mother's earnest efforts to keep her child from harm by obeying her doctor.

The neurological system develops early, like other vital life systems in the fetus. Therefore taking the supplement is essential right away. As soon as she knows she is pregnant, a woman should begin. Some medical advisers insist women should take increased doses from the moment they think they *might* be pregnant, or even when they are hoping to get pregnant. The necessity of consuming folic acid in prenatal vitamins from the earliest possible phase of pregnancy heightens urgency of putting oneself under doctor's protection as early as possible, of activating status as obstetric patient. Knowing you can do something that could change the life of your child is why pregnant women take those vitamins. But even scrupulous care in taking those vitamins will not guarantee fetal health. Lots of things can go wrong. The value of the vitamins themselves is mostly visible when they are lacking and something goes wrong, rather than showing clear proof of themselves as reasons for healthy pregnancy outcomes.

Wondering what else there might be to do to assist the coming child inclines women to follow even prenatal instructions that seem silly or overcautious. Broader lessons about prenatal care can be drawn here. Warnings about folic acid teach women to do these things: to seek out new medical care, buy vitamins, and ingest them. Ingesting them itself feels like an event. Prenatal vitamins are notoriously large, a big pill to choke down when one's gag reflex is strong. Women take hold of the vitamins with big glass of water as a sort of charm to protect baby from harm. I suspect most women do not have their own good uppermost in mind when trying to force that pill down the gullet, but the good of the baby: do this and he will live.

## Collaborations in Pregnancy

The instructions an obstetrician gives begin to shape pregnancy as a coherent work. The protocols of prenatal care resemble a job description, coming to a first OB visit like clocking in for one's first shift. Since the early twentieth century, women in the United States have been advised to choose a doctor to see them through pregnancy. Some women opt for a nurse or midwife, but the vast majority of American pregnancies have been overseen by doctors since the mid-twentieth century. The pregnant woman's doctor, as one sassy 1940s manual suggests, becomes "Boss of your Life." Early twentieth-century guidebooks remind women that medical care would only get results if women got good at following orders, since "doctors can give the full benefits of their skill only to those women who do their part by following instructions faithfully week after week, throughout nine months." Early twenty-first-century manuals keep up this refrain, with Dr. Michael Roizen and Dr. Mehmet Oz explaining, "the doctors will help you de-stress as they describe accurately and rationally what happens during a thrilling nine months of life." The causal links among authority, obedience, and consequences here are clear. First, a woman concedes that the doctor has knowledge necessary for successful pregnancy, second, that this knowledge spells out her nine months' work, and third, that obedience promises some measurable results upon the baby's birth.[3]

Given doctors' status as authorities over pregnancy, with few other contestants for that office in the experience of many women, a doctor now may not be only "Boss" but may stand in for other important offices in the life of the patient: translator, prophet, confessor. Because doctors came to seem the only authority competent to interpret pregnancy accurately, many questions about pregnancy get brought to doctors. Some of these are not strictly medical. Advice literature from the early twentieth century on invites these questions, promoting the expertise of doctors and disparaging that from other communities, especially female ones maligned as gossipy. The "modern" woman is supposed to defer to the former and dismiss the latter. By the middle of the last century, making one's doctor "Boss of your Life" became a way of proving oneself up to date, declaring independence from the outdated customs handed down by women. In the 1950s a working mother-to-be, Ellen Raymond, expressed her "first joyful intimation that the processes of pregnancy were not rigid and inflexible, fixed by the taboos and injunctions handed down by generations of nonprofessional authorities on the subject, i.e.: relatives and friends." Raymond's wording addresses traditional pregnancy manners in a negative way.

Her words suggest culture sets "taboos and injunctions" that make the experience appear unchanging, while doctors turn biological understanding into a new way of doing pregnancy that appears timeless, outside of culture.[4]

Again and again maternity guides from this period urge readers to shun the advice that comes from mothers, grandmothers, relatives, neighbors, sisters, and in some cases, to avoid those people altogether during pregnancy. Guides profess that reducing worries is their primary motive, since old wives' tales are liable to scare the mother with superstitions disproved by modern medicine. This advice removes pregnancy from the sphere of informal authorities and installs professional medicine as authority instead. Women earnest to do well in pregnancy may compare notes with other peers, but must look to their chosen medical attendant to spell out their duties. Orders to do something to help make the baby well assume that it is within a mother's power to make the baby well—which, historically, has not always been what experts thought. While some critics cringe at its imposition of social control over women, the very logic of prenatal care takes quite a positive view of women's capacity to act. As Drs. Roizen and Oz explain in their pregnancy manual, "Once you see some of the long-term effects you can have on the health of your child while you're pregnant, you'll realize that it's important to start this process with the end goal in mind." Women's actions improve chances of fetal well-being but are not guaranteed to do more than that. Still, pregnant women have to act in faith that what they are doing will help the baby.[5]

As a woman takes up actions expected of her, childbearing takes on the character of work. Women may measure the work of carrying a fetus most sensitively through the exhaustion that comes from doing it. Especially in the first few months, pregnant women complain of tiredness, often articulated in superlatives: so tired, bone-tired, wiped out. A woman taking up other work during pregnancy does so while hard at work assisting the building of another's body. The flourishing of the coming child, even the very life of the child, depends on the woman's acting in a certain way. Others can help *her*, by providing the woman with food, rest, aid. But all other assistance intended for the baby has to come through the woman. Outsiders only can really help the baby through the body of the mother. No one else can do for the growing baby what the woman who carries the child does. Others may help the fetus while she is carrying, but not directly, only through her.[6]

Nevertheless, the work of gestation is not only the woman's private labor but a collaboration. She alone can do some of the things required in childbearing but in many cases she does not act alone. As biology has made obvious, growing a baby represents a sort of coworking of the mother and the father of a child. Sometimes maternity manuals go big in naming collaborators, observing that a woman is working together with nature or God in the creation of a child. Advice writers in religious traditions describe the parental couple as working with God in the making of a new human being. In an important mid-twentieth-century address, Pope Pius XII reminds Italian midwives of their high calling helping with "this admirable collaboration of the parents, of nature and of God, from which is born a new human being in the image and likeness of God." A Catholic prenatal care manual counsels pregnant women to "feel pride that God has chosen you to participate with Him in creating a human being with the potentialities of sainthood." The expectant woman's participation in this collaboration is visible, in agreeing to have her body be the site of growth and delivery, in contributing oxygen, energy, foodstuffs to the project, and in recognizing the presence of the child.[7]

By taking the many steps prescribed in prenatal care, a woman acts rather than proceeding passively for nine months. The culture of reproductive choice makes a woman's action volitional, a choice to carry to term, even for women who would never choose to terminate their pregnancies. Wide availability of contraception and abortion, plus social sanction to employ both to control when and whether sexual activity makes a baby, makes childbearing a conscious choice. The woman's willingness to let the child develop spurs action. General assumptions about reproduction shape the experience of individuals, especially in a pregnant woman's encounter with reproductive medicine and her decisions to follow the directives that will support the health of the baby she plans to birth. The accomplishment of a full-term pregnancy, as it is supposed to be enacted according to current customs of prenatal care, is not merely a result of the involuntary process of a woman's body. Indeed the whole premise of prenatal care rebels against old views that attributed successful gestation to natural or instinctive process. In the turn from nineteenth to twentieth centuries, pregnancy advice writers strove to explain what women might be adding to the project that man, embryo, God, and nature already had going.[8]

Emphasizing the voluntary and active character of childbearing, Carolyn Van Blarcom opens her manual with a swipe at those, men in particular, who fail to respect the labors of pregnant women and erroneously assume baby-making is instinctual and automatic. She urges her female readers to persuade husbands that their "bearing and rearing children merits quite the same thoughtful attention as his work, to which he devotes his best powers." Careful though men might be in their own occupations, Van Blarcom reflects, "as to childbearing, if they thought of it at all, they looked upon it as simply one of those natural functions which always had and doubtless always would take care of itself."[9]

## Acting: How a Pregnant Woman Works

Most obstetricians and the expectant couples they serve now would accept Van Blarcom's premise. A woman's activity in pregnancy presupposes her decision to do it and consists in conscious choices to assist the functioning of her body to support the baby's growth. However, the acts involved in childbearing do not meet a clear metric of success. Why should a woman do all of the things prenatal care urges her to do, if the doing may or may not yield what was, in the early twentieth century, unblushingly called a "better baby"? The language of maternity manuals sometimes runs hyperbolic and favors sports or military metaphors. Minnie Randell's prenatal exercises are likened to "the same light drill as for the soldier," since they discipline mothers in self-control, which in labor "will give that confidence that is half the battle." Kathleen Vaughan compares the pregnant woman to "an athlete in need of training for her special job." The sports metaphor is problematic, since first prize cannot necessarily be pledged to the healthy-eating, clean-living mom. The quality of the effort women invest does not guarantee quality "outcome." Cyril Pink's guide boldly argues that "[e]xperience shows that any woman whose productive power is high enough to allow of conception can produce a healthy baby, provided she manages her pregnancy the right way." Pink's words make a woman's prenatal management—diet, exercise, good behavior—responsible for the baby's health. Rules hand down thou-shalls and shalt-nots as though everything matters, even as rule-makers admit that healthy children sometimes come to careless parents and that parents who do all sometimes have children with serious problems. Rather than reversing patterns of blame from antique embryology— women contributing nothing but likely to cause ruin—current views make judgment harsher, prompting women to claim guilt for what was done or left undone.[10]

Admitting that each pregnancy is unique, early twentieth-century doctor Josephine Baker advises that "observance of the outline of the hygiene of pregnancy which has been given will almost always result in a normal pregnancy, and the avoidance of any serious complications." Stakes are high for observing that "outline." Because prenatal care half-promises that improved outcomes will follow good behavior, it invites (obligates?) women to trace fetal problems to their misbehavior. Theologian L. Serene Jones regrets the way a friend wracked her memory after suffering a miscarriage: "'What did I do to make this happen? . . . Was it that cigarette I smoked last Saturday? The glass of wine I had three weeks ago? Did I not take the right vitamins?'" The promises of prenatal care pinch women in a double bind. Things that might go wrong are and always have been outside the mother's control. Roizen and Oz reassure, "while there's no guarantee for a 100 percent perfect birth, you can take comfort in the fact that many health issues are genetically predetermined and not something for which you should accept blame." Not something for which you should accept blame: that is, in cases where things go wrong, there may be nothing the woman can do to avert the harm, but she has to act anyway as though she can, since her "job is to optimize the fetal environment." Such a pronouncement both exonerates and threatens. A woman may not be able to avert disaster and cannot claim credit for what goes right, but has to act as though both were true.[11]

"Labor" is the word we use for the process of getting the baby out. It is not too much of a stretch to apply words like "work" and "labor" to pregnancy too, if tentatively, with reservations. Pregnancy is most emphatically not just another kind of labor, and some may appropriately hesitate to call it work. Comparing "reproductive labor" to other sorts of productive labor in order to make it count in that way errs too. Childbearing is not work in that sense, not production of another copy of a thing or (at least not directly) expanding the pool of human resources. Against such a view of reproduction, Lisa Guenther's words are powerful: "The birth of any given child has never happened before and will never happen again; as such, it resists both expectation and exact repetition." It makes sense to speak of pregnancy as resembling work only with qualification. Emphasis here is more on the active quality of the tasks, rather than on the character of those tasks as product-making or remunerative.[12]

The requirements of pregnancy sometimes have pitted it against other sorts of work deemed appropriate for women. In the past, pregnant women have been excluded from many jobs and even from some household labors from fears that their condition would ruin the beer or the butter. In theory, Americans now recognize that women can do both things at once, work at a job and gestate a baby, with no harm caused to either undertaking by the other. In practice, the work of gestation often gets underemphasized. In the United States now, pregnant women work in jobs nearly up to their delivery dates mostly with cultural approval. Women doing jobs ably can demonstrate that pregnancy does not interfere with their *real* work. In 1951 Ellen Raymond was proud to report in a woman's magazine that she got away with working "till my baby was born" by concealing the situation for most of the months because she knew that her "value to the organization would cease with that knowledge." Such pressure is now frowned upon. Job discrimination against pregnant women persists but is prosecutable. The bargain often plays out this way: acting as though pregnancy is as nothing, no obstacle to employment, is an expedient allowing women to keep their day jobs instead of being scuttled. That bargain is premised on the falsehood that carrying a baby takes little work of its own.[13]

People in other times may have prevented women's employment from phobia about the belly. What we now know about what is happening might not only bless continued employment during pregnancy but also heighten regard for this internal work. *Homo faber* knowingly collaborates in the making of *homo sapiens* there in the belly. Part of the work of pregnancy is understanding what it is. We do ourselves wrong, individually and collectively, if we persist in misunderstanding childbearing or failing to give it thought at all. Seeing rightly requires attention to what we see.

## Showing: What a Pregnant Woman Witnesses

Childbearing is a showing forth in two senses. In the first, a woman witnesses something shown in a singular way to her alone. In the second, the woman shows something to others about how humans come to be.

Today, when the basics of fetal development are common knowledge, consciousness about pregnancy is a big part of being pregnant. One scholar quips that for American women pregnancy "is constructed as a reading assignment." The ability to *know* that one is carrying a baby is a distinguishing feature of what it is like now to carry one. "Every prospective mother should find it of great interest to learn about the organs of reproduction . . . about the development also of the baby to be," Minnie Randell maintains. Expectant mothers simultaneously can know in scientific terms what happens inside the body and also know that this account explains what is happening to *them*. A great deal about what develops in the fetus day to day is now common knowledge. A woman carrying a baby can map her private internal experience against the general model: since the human fetus grows eyelashes around week eighteen, my fetus must be growing eyelashes today. The mere fact of knowledge does not determine what one ought to do with it, though. Pregnancy is not self-interpreting, even to those in the throes of it.[14]

From the early twentieth century some advice-givers insistently urged their readers to understand what was going on. This advice has been offered on the premise that increased understanding reduces anxiety. Knowledge became the pregnant woman's duty, the means by which she would root out her own superstitions and the better follow doctors' orders. Because doctors worried that maternal worry could cause its own pregnancy problems, women were told that they needed knowledge to allay fears and find motivation to follow care instructions. Good cheer could spring from awareness of the basic facts about pregnancy, the woman taking "natural pleasure in the knowledge that her body nurtures and protects the young life which, later, is to appear in all perfection." However, prenatal care manuals may themselves propagate some superstitions and strange beliefs.[15]

Knowing what is going on also can raise fears of what can go wrong. Fetal development is within a mother's understanding now, but its unfolding remains outside her control. This problem, that more knowledge can generate more worry, comes through in maternity manuals. Drs. Roizen and Oz spend some time presenting pregnancy as something automatic, a machinery that moves of its own accord: "Most of the time, your job is just to get out of the way and let this remarkable process work naturally." Yet, the very existence of a hefty book like theirs and many others, packed with information and illustrations for the middle-educated pregnant reader, seems to assume just the opposite: that a woman cannot and should not "just get out of the way," but must *know* what is going on and *do* something about it. More knowledge is offered as a solution to a problem created by a little knowledge. "Knowledge is the best defense," Drs. Oz and Roizen insist. Their book gives women information in order to "reinforce our 'just say know' mantra. As knowledge goes down, anxiety goes up. If you can flip those trajectories, you'll feel much better about some of the issues you may be facing." As advice writers must realize, learning more is just as likely to increase worry as reduce it. If a woman knows nothing about how pregnancy proceeds and is assured by doctors that all will work out fine, she has nothing to worry about. If, on the other hand, she knows quite a bit about all the things that can go wrong, it is entirely reasonable that she would worry. She might worry a lot. In our own time pregnancy advice writers tend to bring knowledge and worry full circle in a way that reinforces the authority of the obstetrician's office. If women, with worries and curiosity raised, need further advice they should turn to their health care providers.[16]

Doctors' conclusions that women would misunderstand pregnancy and become worried is, contrariwise, also a reason some offer in advising against the pregnant woman's knowing too much. Some writers scold women not to think about pregnancy but to rest assured that doctors are doing the thinking for them. Because doctors understand things patients do not, women should "ask *him* your questions, *not* your friends at the bridge table." Indeed some writers counsel that once they learn the basics, expectant women should think as little as possible about what might be going on inside the body. As Nicholson Eastman soothes, "the woman who cultivates a certain oblivion to the fact that she is pregnant (although obeying the ordinary rules of diet and hygiene) does much better than her introspective sister." Entrusting comprehension instead to the experts, women should get on with life while the baby goes chugging along according to doctors' orders.[17]

I side with the introspective sister: it seems eminently right for a woman to ponder the fact of the fetus there under her skin. Just as the pregnant woman is singularly positioned to perform some particular goods for the fetus, the woman alone experiences the presence of a coming human being when she does and in the way she does. Pregnancy affords unique access to the knowledge of another human through interactions of thought and feeling. Awareness of fetal presence comes through fetal "kicks" and through her own changing shape; her levels of energy, nausea, and attentiveness; her altered balance, disposition, patterns of thought. No one else, even the father of the child, experiences the new person directly. As Iris Marion Young names it, a mother has a "privileged relation" to the other life that is within her body.[18]

The pregnant woman holds concealed a human being never before existing in the world, a new creature. Her privileged relation is not only a matter of firsts. James Mumford recognizes how significant this is: "it's not just that the mother is first to get wind of the newone's presence," not only that she has an "information premium." She has a special relationship to the knowledge of the coming baby, to the coming baby itself, and to the achievement of her body in bearing. We become ourselves through another, and we first learn of each other through another. Beyond the fact of its fiction, what Mumford faults about the myth of storks is that in it the baby "is brought to both [mother and father] at the same time," a mistake that hides "from view the fact that, compared to the mother, everybody else, including even the father, always remain at one remove." Children do not just appear, but appear only after nine month's residence with one to whom they appeared first.[19]

Describing the "newone's presence" and a woman's initial awareness of it opens a question long puzzling to philosophers and scientists alike: When does this concealed being become a person? Or, as the older literature preferred to phrase the question, when does the fetus gain a human soul? Arguments about this timing, whether named ensoulment or hominization, persist. Discouragingly, much of the question gets absorbed into polemics about the treatment of embryos, reproductive technologies, and abortion. Perhaps legal interest in ensoulment must stick around abortion or embryo manipulation controversies. But because attention has been directed that way, discussion about the more usual circumstance—the norm, the expectation for successful pregnancies, a stage in the life of all brought to birth—regrettably has been muted. This is too bad, because the approximate time and actual place of that event are so important. Ordinary men and women might decide it does not make much practical difference exactly when the hoped-for fetus becomes a person, because it is hard to know with precision when the fetus started. A conscientious layperson might be forgiven for thinking that deciding when life begins only matters in hard cases.[20]

Philosophers may never agree on the instant when a group of cells becomes a person. Attention to this question, regrettably but perhaps not surprisingly, often treats it literally out of context. Those arguing over when the embryo becomes recognizably human sometimes overlook the location where many agree this transformation occurs: in utero. That event occurs in the body of the woman. If *when* it happens remains a mystery, *where* it happens is obvious. The woman is a sort of unique audience for the event, the only other person physically present when ensoulment happens, whenever and however it happens. Thinking about how an embryo gets a soul is an appropriate activity for somebody who is carrying an embryo in her abdomen. Maternity advice givers in early modern Germany described childbearing as a kind of craft work. God's creation of a new person was a kind of redoing, in miniature, the creation of the whole world. This man-as-microcosm idea places the pregnant woman as the one singled out to behold this work. The mother cannot see ensoulment but she is no less a singular witness to its occurrence. One way of witnessing it is tactile. "Quickening" in former eras was roundly considered proof that a baby *was.* Those who assume the soul is transmitted by the father or spontaneously generates through genetic combination have enough reason to be impressed at that fact, that this coming to life happens in the female body. Those who assume God directly infuses the soul into each human being should hardly be able to contain their delighted astonishment at what is implied. To believe that God gives every person a soul, directly and individually, is to believe that each pregnant woman is host to a kind of visitation from God, is honored as audience and collaborator, a watcher at a holy place, attending God doing something new. She is present at this creation.[21]

It is an astonishing occupation, carrying around embodied knowledge and a creature. The pregnant woman gets the revelation first. Seeing her, others observe a sizable work of caretaking entrusted to a particular person. The rest of us wait to encounter the new person for the first time. The expectant woman is not waiting in the same way. She already has encountered the new person. She already knows something.

It might be objected that with the advent of fetal imaging others *do* behold the baby as immediately as does the mother. Others, as in the case of the ultrasound technician, see the baby perhaps better and before the mother does so. In a routine ultrasound appointment in a wanted, normal pregnancy, the images are made available equally and simultaneously to mother and father and any others in the room. Mothers about to undergo an ultrasound during pregnancy sometimes are asked, "Are you excited to meet your baby?" "Meeting" the baby this way, the image is given to the pregnant woman through persons and machines outside of her. The revelation comes in spite of her, through a tool that bypasses the opacity of her skin and organs in order to show the fetal figure. Onlookers rely on the technician to help them "see."

What do you see in an ultrasound? Much has been written analyzing ultrasound images, often criticizing their misuse or their focus on the abstracted fetus. Barbara Katz Rothman faults doctors for "think[ing] of fetuses as separate patients more or less trapped within the maternal environment." In general, criticism along these lines charges that sonograms provide images of the hidden fetus blotting out the flesh of the mother. The machine allows viewers to see the baby by looking right past the mother. When quickening was the way mothers and others knew a baby was on the way, sense of touch trumped sight in ascertaining the presence of a baby. Fetal imaging reverses this tradition.[22]

Ultrasound images can be helpful but they are not simply so. They give expectant parents different kinds of information. They may provide a kind of proof of pregnancy. For many parents the chief use of ultrasound images is providing reassurance that the baby is not in danger or helping to understand physical problems. Another important use of sonography is to discover the sex of the child. In any case, the role of images is not mostly to introduce a woman to her baby. In best case scenarios, with a sonographer catching the fetus at good angles and finding good health, what parents see is pretty indeterminate, darkish lumpy outlines of flesh with prominent dots and dashes of bone. Even high definition ultrasounds do not really show what your baby looks like. The power of the visual image demotes women's sense of touch as a means of perceiving the fetus.

A 2015 television commercial sponsored by Huggies diapers highlights this conundrum. The commercial features a thirty-year-old

Brazilian woman named Tatiana "meeting" her son in utero in an ultrasound, with this emotional twist: Tatiana lost her eyesight at age seventeen. Because she is blind she cannot see an ultrasound of her baby. The scene moves to a clinical exam room, where a doctor reports the fetal heartbeat. Tatiana asks him to describe her baby. Then the sonographer presents her with a 3-D printout of her fetus's face. He asks, "Is this what you imagine?" He says, "That's your son." She unwraps the molded model and "sees" it by touching it with her hands. The gesture is not just a tear-jerker for Tatiana and her audience, it is a powerful illustration of the shifting relative importance of sight and touch for engaging one's baby-to-be.[23]

Parents' desire to see their baby may encourage them to make more of the picture than it truly shows, to be awfully forgiving of that snapshot because they want the picture to reveal more than it can. As Rebecca Kukla argues, reflecting on twenty-first-century ubiquity of those from-the-womb pictures, what fetal imaging mostly serves to do is to superimpose a generic image of a fetus on one's perception of the hidden, private, actual fetus, "your baby." Even after a woman has dismounted from the sonography table, she continues to imagine a baby inside of her looking that way because she has seen pictures resembling generic babies at similar developmental stages.[24]

A mother must wait until birth, like everyone else, to "meet her baby" face to face. A pregnant woman's witness to the becoming of a new person comes through senses other than sight, through the experience of the body. In order for a person to come into the world, a woman has to bear the fetus. She holds and beholds the person first. The woman enjoys a unique witness to the coming of a new person, but all who have chance to observe the fact that women walk around the streets bearing life, behold that to which she bears witness.[25]

## Witness: What the Pregnant Woman Shows

A pregnant woman provides living, breathing evidence of something essential about our humanity, reminding us of some things we might be prone to forget. Above all, observing pregnancy underscores our dependence. We come from each other. In the lovely figure of speech favored by Rothman, we "unfold" from each other. On ordinary days we might realize that is true in a general way, understand our place as a species connected to others, our fellowship on the globe with other animals, our place in the cosmos, and so on. But childbearing shows this connection as not merely a general truth but a particular one, that we each come from a particular other. You spent the first, formative part of your life in the body of some particular woman. Dependence, not independence, is the default setting for human existence. Similarly, pregnancy demonstrates that our lives never are really autonomous, self-determined, a composite of free choices that only benefit or injure an individual's private self. Pregnancy presses recognition that our actions bear immediate effect on others, for good and ill, in short and long term. To be sure, in other life situations the causal linkage is much less direct, or direct but much less evident. But pregnant women may learn in emphatic ways a feature of human life on earth—what I do affects you—and observers might as well profit from this reminder. Observers hope that the woman chooses to do things that will be good for the fetus. In many cases, volitionally and not, women do these goods. It is a tall order, quite a thing for humans to expect from each other, that this much generosity must regularly operate in order for the system to go.

The capacity for awareness when carrying and birthing a child is significant. Humans sometimes feel this significance the wrong way around, finding the concept powerful not in itself but as a way of decoding something else, claiming pregnancy as metaphor for things construed as more important than pregnancy. Cynthia Coe regrets this mistake as far back as Plato, recalling in Plato's *Symposium* that a character named Diotima admires the offspring of philosophical conversation more than offspring from human bodies. Fruitful conversation helps "give birth to what he has been carrying inside him for ages," ideas, fruit of a "firmer bond of friendship" than the parents of human children because these "children" are "more beautiful and more immortal." Ideas, which men can gestate and birth, are more important and desirable than the actual children with whom women are pregnant. Coe argues that this metaphor of birth works through devaluation of actual birth.[26]

The simple fact of a woman with a visible pregnant bump presents a complex testimony about the nature of our lives. If you think about it. But you could also not think about it. This thinking changes both the way one experiences and the way others observe pregnancy. Many times and peoples preferred not to think about it much at all, from modesty or shame or lack of comprehension or conviction that gestation, being the lot of the inferior sex, did not merit very much thought. Or that that condition only deserved reflection in a scientific sort of way. Even Nicholson Eastman, a leader in developing popularized prenatal care in mid-twentieth-century America, leaves the thinking up to doctors.

But women who walk around with this peculiar thing happening to them might be better off to not leave the thinking up to their doctors. Furthermore, observers, though deferring to a woman's own sense of what is happening, might clear a little head space for this mystery too. Not only at birth but in childbearing, the witness of the woman with child communicates in a "semi-public" way our mutual dependence, participation in creation, and invitation to charity.

# 4

# *Protecting and Providing*

Your doctor will help you as much as he can with your meal planning but this part of your prenatal care is your special responsibility. You have every reason to feel proud when you make a good job of it.

—US Children's Bureau, *Prenatal Care* (1962)


The risk of injury to the baby by a fall is very slight. He is so wonderfully well protected that only a *very* serious fall can do harm.

—Cyril V. Pink, *The Foundations of Motherhood* (1947)

S tuart Blakely, early twentieth-century New York obstetrician, shared with his colleagues the "superstitions" collected in five years' service in an "average American industrial city"—where, the good doctor carefully notes, the "ignorant and foreign born have no monopoly" on odd beliefs. Chalking taboos up to belief in ancient magic and "primitive" ideas about women, the doctor observed folk beliefs that mostly intended protection from harm. Though some people thought "[w]eighing the mother will make the baby daring," danger was the noteworthy feature of most other actions. The expectant mother's bathing could put the fetus in peril of future drowning. Coitus could kill the fetus. A woman could strangle the fetus by holding her arms up over her head or walking under a clothesline. A woman's experience of a shock could stain the baby or cause miscarriage.[1]

Though the body in pregnancy acts in a range of ways, many tasks can be sorted into two categories: protection and provision. Most prenatal care instructions charge women to do things to keep the fetus from harm, and also to supply the fetus with food. To do so well, the woman has to act. A childbearing woman simultaneously provides to the fetus shelter, food, and clothing and is herself those things to the child.

### Protecting Baby from World and Self

A fetus resting in a fluid bubble in a tight-sealed barrel of muscle sunk deep in the body enjoys thick insulation between itself and the world. That protective cover does not only belong to another person; it *is* another person. A good word must first be given to systems that the female body is able, on its own without volition, to construct or adapt when prompted by the signal of the embryo's hormones. The pregnant woman actively can enhance what fetal protections come automatically. While pregnant women in the nineteenth century were likelier thought to be in delicate condition, frail and sickly, by the middle of the twentieth century, many doctors began to present pregnancy as a period of robust health. Medicine proclaims that the pregnant woman is formidable in the edifice of walls, barriers, filters, and climate controls she interposes between baby and the world. She serves as sentry and bodyguard, fortress and sanctuary. Protection is the first service a woman performs for baby, the maintenance of safety in a place.

In addition to the unconscious protections the maternal body affords, conscious efforts to shield the baby from harm become part of the pregnant woman's way of life. She is instructed to not wear garments that bind the belly, and to avoid shoes that could make her tip over, precarious heights or climbs, unsteady stairs, or high stools to keep the baby from falls. If she falls, it is her body that absorbs the blow for the baby. She is also to rid herself of poisons and avoid toxins, which sometimes requires that she change jobs. To a limited degree, workplace regulations applied to pregnant women are concerned with the woman's health, but even more they are efforts to require the woman to shield the fetus from harm. The starting point of prenatal maternity behavior is avoiding harm where possible, and where unavoidable, putting oneself between the fetus and what might hurt. Coming between these involuntary and volitional guards is the placenta. Much lore attaches to this organ, considered by some ancients to be a "second self" or external soul for a fetus, or kin, like a sibling. The placenta belongs to woman and fetus together, is built up by the embryo when cells divide in the early weeks after conception. It serves as a fastener, linking the fetus to the uterine wall. It serves as a filter, drawing oxygen and nutrients from the mother's blood. It serves as a waste disposal portal, channeling excreta back out to the body of the mother to be removed.[2]

From antiquity, the placenta has been respected as a potent, even magical, thing. The expulsion of it is part of labor, for many an anti-climactic stage when the baby is already out and mother might be exalted or exhausted. Once out, the placenta is not mere medical waste. People have ceremonially buried or burned placentas, used them in witchcraft, even eaten them, a fad recently revived. Its mystery stems from its peculiar character, a liminal organ between mother and child and existing only during gestation. Substances pass through it from mother to fetus and vice versa. Earlier embryology imagined the fetus sealed off from the pollutions of the woman's guts. In the twentieth century, this misunderstanding yielded sorry consequences, as the placenta proved able after all to transmit toxins from maternal blood to the child. Doctors prescribed medications for pregnant women that caused birth defects. The placenta turns out to be more a "bloody sieve" than impenetrable barrier.[3]

The flip side of a woman's unique access to the forming fetus is her unique position to do harm. The placenta is part of the system enabling a mother to prevent perils generated by her own body from reaching the fetus. This is among the most worry-fraught features of pregnancy: a woman not only has to protect the fetus from dangers outside but also from her own self. Harm to the fetus can be afflicted intentionally, inadvertently, or even against one's own will—as when a mother's illness or immune response wreaks damage on the fetus. This is the case with rubella, or German measles, an epidemic of which struck the United States in the 1960s. Americans were dismayed to find that rubella caused a rash and mild fever in mothers, but a range of problems including blindness and deafness, cognitive and other injuries in the babies born to mothers who were sick with it. More recently, the global outbreak of the Zika virus causes alarm, injuring fetuses of women who get sick from it.[4]

Danger from mother to baby can come not only from disease but from digestion. Just as early advocates of prenatal care enjoined expectant women that their good diets could improve fetal health, they cautioned that a woman's risky habits or poor diet could poison her children. Cyril Pink traces some incidents of miscarriage to the "poisoning of the body" from "wrong habits of life." Pink primarily worries that by eating processed or "flesh" food (meat), a woman unwitting collects in her body toxins that could kill the baby. Even constipation can be a sign of a woman's failure, retention of poisons that she should have removed through fiber and "vital foods." Because prenatal care tasks women with repelling harm, any dangers that the fetus does encounter sometimes have been read as the woman's mistakes. Childbearing is not inherently dangerous, Pink indicates, but only becomes so if the mother neglects protective duties: a mother's physical failings can turn into moral failings. Birth defects have been read as judgments on the bearing woman's way of life.[5]

The protective function of pregnancy has been understood in part as the need to defend a woman's offspring from her very self. In folk traditions, childbearing women consistently have attracted more credit for harms inflicted than for benefits rendered. When doctors in the nineteenth and early twentieth centuries began heaping scorn on theories of maternal impression, they had very little else to offer as alternative explanation for markings and defects. Belief in maternal impressions was the gateway superstition to a host of others. *Modeling for Motherhood*, for instance, takes aim at them, assuring, "In the first place, you know that having a nightmare won't mean that Junior will be wearing a horse-shaped birthmark." That "first place" opens the lists of presumably ridiculous beliefs the authors also wish to deny: that having a baby over age thirty is bad because muscles are too hard and bones won't yield, that every child would cost a tooth, that heartburn predicts a hairy baby, that smelling fresh paint might cause premature birth, or that stooping or stretching one's arms could strangle the baby: "Don't do that! You'll tie the cord around its neck!" Nurse-midwives serving in rural Kentucky with the Frontier Nursing Service in the early twentieth century confronted similar folk beliefs about birth, such as the requirement of teas or spices during hard labor, "cording the leg," having verses read from the Bible to the laboring woman, or having an axe put under the mother's bed. Writing during World War II, Castallo and Walz remind, "Nothing the mother-to-be experiences emotionally will have any effect on the infant's development. The mother can haunt the art galleries and the concert halls without improving her unborn child any more than a visit to the chamber of horrors will harm him. She can take a two-headed calf or a double concerto in her stride."[6]

If these superstitions were so preposterous, why did maternity manuals bother even to name them? Listing them facilitates a shift of authority. Guides acknowledge that women might hear such rumors from the sort of people to whom they otherwise would turn for advice: friends, relatives, other women telling their own pregnancy stories. Trading women's lore for doctors' counsel means requiring a different kind of proof for believable information about the body. "Where are the statistical tables on which old wives base their predictions?" demand the authors of *Modeling for Motherhood*. Right answers about pregnancy and fetal development only can come from the right people, the experts. So if you "wouldn't let an amateur tinker with your wrist watch," these writers aver, you should not "let one influence your peace of mind."[7]

The importance of the woman's fetal protective function gets highlighted when set against a woman's other concurrent works. Sometimes the job of carrying a baby competes with those. In order to remove the fetus from danger related to their work, women sometimes have had to leave jobs, losing income by their own choice or by another's. A landmark expression of Progressive labor regulation, *Muller v. Oregon* articulated the US Supreme Court's support for childbearing labor. The 1908 decision upheld an Oregon law limiting the working hours of pregnant women, which laundry owner Curt Muller violated in allowing an expectant woman to do a shift longer than ten hours. The court deemed woman's procreative contribution more valuable than her mere laundering. Recognizing that a woman's "performance of maternal functions place her at a disadvantage in the struggle for subsistence," Chief Justice Josiah Brewer nevertheless declared that "as healthy mothers are essential to vigorous offspring, the physical well being of woman becomes an object of public interest and care in order to preserve the strength and vigor of the race." This ruling protected women by constraining their workforce participation. The 1978 Pregnancy Discrimination Act, a new provision of Title VII of the Civil Rights Act of 1964, forbids penalizing pregnant women in employment, but admits the work of fetal care sometimes should take priority. Women should not be shut out of jobs because of pregnancy, but still may be motivated or required to protect the growing fetus by staying away from heavy lifting, hazardous chemicals, gases, or physical force that might cause fetal injury.[8]

Lacking recourse to the idioms of the early twentieth century, twenty-first-century writers struggle to describe this maternal work of fetal protection. In a 2015 decision, *Young v. United Parcel Service,* justices' language floundered between contemning favored status and respecting the social good of gestational work. In this case, the court decided that UPS employee Peggy Young had a legitimate discrimina-tion claim due to her pregnancy. Expecting a baby in 2006 and under medical counsel not to lift packages heavier than twenty pounds, Young requested temporary assignment to light duty. She was refused and placed on unpaid leave, losing her medical coverage. The court major-ity decreed Young's discrimination suit valid. In a dissenting opinion, Justice Kennedy acknowledges that pregnant women who find their regular work impossible during pregnancy must take "necessary steps to avoid risks to their health and the health of their future children. This is why the difficulties pregnant women face in the workplace are and do remain an issue of national importance." Justice Kennedy is perhaps to be commended for effort to recognize the common good involved in pregnancy. Job discrimination persists against pregnant women. Doubtless more aware of the impact of prenatal behavior on women and children, twenty-first-century American judges might be less comfortable than their forerunners in using language that treats motherhood as a woman's civic duty.[9]

Jobs that require heavy lifting pose challenges to pregnancy, but white-collar office work can generate challenges too. Daily office stress can do harm, whether for women in high-powered professions or in low-paying employment. Epigenetics, the study of environmental fac-tors shaping the expression of genes, indicates that the maternal "envi-ronment" and not only genes contribute to lifelong health or debility of offspring. Reducing stress thus becomes another protective task of pregnancy. Not only in preparation for delivery but for good gesta-tion, Minnie Randell exhorts "practicing the art of relaxation," with deep breathing and imaginative exercises, since "[t]raining of the mind should receive as much attention during pregnancy as the training of the muscles." Some defense is needful for the other stresses beyond workplace ones that can wreak harm on fetus through mother. The stress inflicted by racism in the United States, a 2018 study revealed, is baneful to mothers: African American women and babies suffer birth-related complications at higher rates than white women, even women at similar levels of income and education. Stresses accumulated in a woman's life can cause physical hurt to her offspring. Thus pregnant women must engage in complex protective tasks. The job assigned pregnant women to "optimize" the fetal environment is no light work, one requiring discernment of dangers inside and out, actual and potential.[10]

Beyond the physical dangers that could come to mother and baby, spiritual perils threaten too. Pregnancy in past centuries was counted a mentally and spiritually sensitive phase. The temperamental uterus was thought to cause maternal mania, nineteenth-century doctors worrying over women struck by "insanity of pregnancy." From the Middle Ages on, involvement in the process of bringing forth new life was thought to place women in proximity of spiritual powers, good or evil. Historian Susan Karant-Nunn notes that men in the Middle Ages recognized women's unique status as birth approached: "Their wives dreamed unaccustomed dreams, were moody, and yearned for special foods. Such behavior was sufficient evidence to both sexes that women were more than normally susceptible to the Devil's influence." Therefore, because pregnant women were subject to these dangers, the Roman Catholic church in the Middle Ages devised rites designed to protect women and their communities from evil. The "churching" of women after childbirth sought to support and restore women weeks after delivery. The rituals were attractive to many, as Karant-Nunn explains, because "[p]regnant women found it credible that they were vulnerable to Satan as they underwent the strange transformation of pregnancy; they consented to avoid church, animals, fields, and water sources after giving birth. . . . Pregnancy cast women into a status fraught with uncertainty, and society expressed its ambivalence in religious as well as secular terms."[11]

The churching ceremony grew out of a medieval practice marking the feast of the presentation of the Virgin Mary. Churching administered a blessing to a woman upon reentry to church life several weeks after she delivered. As the rite developed in German-speaking lands from the twelfth century, the woman would be met at the door of her home by the midwife and women who had been present at delivery. They would make a procession to the door of the church, whereupon a priest would meet the woman, sprinkle her with holy water, then lead the group to the altar. This candle-bearing procession might circle several times, the new mother finally placing a gift at the altar. The ceremony resembled a purity rite, even though Christian belief did not declare women impure through childbirth, as church authorities repeatedly clarified. Women did not need the special blessing because they were unclean but because their participation in the crucial acts of ushering in new life might expose them to evil forces. Through the Reformation, many Protestants retained a version of churching even as they cast out other rituals associated with Roman Catholicism.[12]

Catholics and Protestants both recognized that women carrying babies deserve prayer. Expectant mothers were expected to pray for their children. Women in childbirth sometimes were offered special prayers to help the child out and to protect themselves during that difficult passage. Part of a birth prayer from 1475 implores, "Christ said,

Lazarus come forth. + Christ rules. + Christ calls thee. . . . Ann bore Mary; + Elizabeth, he who went before; +Mary, Our Lord Jesus Christ, without pain and sorrow. Oh infant, whether alive or dead, come forth. + Christ calls thee to the light." Some of these prayers were applied to delivering women in unusual ways. Sometimes prayers adapting Scripture to the particulars of childbirth were placed on the body. They could be carried in an amulet set on the chest. They could be bound to the thigh to draw down the baby: "Lazarus, come out!" Words could be written onto paper and then rinsed into a woman's beverage so she could drink the petition. While some uses of prayer were disapproved by church authorities as superstitious, smacking of charms or incantations, these prayers demonstrate how the work of protection extended throughout pregnancy and into birth.[13]

## Provision

If the job of keeping the child from harm is a pregnant woman's primary negative duty, her eating traditionally has been the most freighted positive aspect of the process. Against the long tradition emphasizing woman's passivity, providing nourishment was singled out as the one activity she must do, and do well. While dietary advice for expectant women usually recommended moderation and variety, counsel on what to eat and drink has changed a lot over time. Three shifts are most prominent. First, older advice on what to eat aimed more directly at the woman's health and less precisely at fetal requirement. Guides from the sixteenth and seventeenth centuries advised pregnant women to eat meat, take a little wine, and avoid foods that made them gassy. A seventeenth-century guide counseled pregnant women to choose foods for "good and wholesome nourishment," and therefore "meats too cold, too hot, and too moist, are to be avoided," along with those too heavily spiced or salted, or "windy" beans and peas. Second, as science in the early twentieth century isolated vitamins and minerals the fetus needed, the expectant mother's task became less a simple feeding and more like requisitioning the tools and raw materials the fetus would need for constructing a body. Third, as birth defects were correlated with the absence or excess of something in the mother's body later in the twentieth century, maternal eating was opened to more scrutiny still, the mother vulnerable to rebuke.[14]

Nineteenth-century findings that calcium ("lime") helped grow teeth and bones, for instance, heightened maternal responsibility for drinking milk. Progressives touted milk as a nearly perfect food, almost magical in its range of benefits. As the twentieth century continued, guides gave more detailed plans, all-day menus, and calorie and vitamin charts for what the pregnant woman was supposed to procure on behalf of her baby. To be sure, many among the intended audience for prenatal care guides may not have started with healthy, varied diets already, owing to poverty or to food traditions.[15]

The *Prenatal Care* booklet published by the US Children's Bureau declares that "it is only through nutrition that the mother is able to influence the child's future." *Prenatal Care* encourages mothers to eat fruits such as "apples, peaches, apricots, pears, oranges, figs, cherries, pineapples, grapes, plums, strawberries, raspberries, or grapefruit," and vegetables including "[o]nions, asparagus, tomatoes, peas, potatoes, lima beans, carrots, string beans, spinach, celery, cress, and lettuce." This bounty is not offered to mother for sake of her enjoyment or nutrients but for fiber—for getting rid of waste products. Excretion is the meeting point of the two primary labors of childbearing, provision and protection.[16]

Ancient and modern advice-givers worried inordinately that women might not be very good at digestion. "The accumulation of waste products in the system is the cause of various minor ailments of pregnancy," the Children's Bureau guide warns. Women should "beware of stuffing yourself with cakes, candy, jelly, pastries, 'soft drinks,' and other 'goodies.'" The mother is supposed to be supplying "the building materials in the form of nutrition" and hauling away the garbage. Advice-givers imply that offering these building materials—and disposing of the runoff—not only affects the physical composition of a child but the child's very character. Especially before popular understanding of genetics began attributing most characteristics to heredity, gestational diet was seen both as an index of the woman's moral character and as her legacy, like a chest full of valuables that she could amass to pass on to her child. In his advocacy for a vegetarian prenatal diet, Cyril Pink declares that "it seems probable that character is influenced by diet." In Pink's observation, children gestated on a vegetarian system grew up "remarkably equable in temper" and "not easily irritated."[17]

The duty of a woman with child is to deliver the right nutritional materials to the emerging baby. From the nineteenth century on, opening her mouth to receive food became an action a woman was to do predominantly for the baby, not for herself. The rightness of food choices was not determined by maternal enjoyment or custom but by acquisition and efficient delivery of materials deemed best for baby. Maternity meal plans are not about "eating for two," women are reprimanded, but eating for one, and that one is not herself. Older advice sometimes hinted at this, Nicholas Culpeper explaining nausea as the result of the fetus having taken the purest of the foodstuffs first and leaving leftovers for the woman's stomach. In some modern guides, morning sickness, however unpleasant it might be for the mother, is regretted predominantly because vomiting deprives the baby of supplies. The fact that pregnant women historically have been credited with this provider's job holds some irony, as being provider was otherwise supposed to be a *father's* chief duty to his family. When industrialization pulled men into a public sphere of paid work and left women's work unpaid at home, men's "breadwinning" was to earn money for dependent wife and children. He provided, she consumed. But the pregnant woman, then and now, offers an image of traditional roles combined into one, both provider and nurturer.[18]

Maternity eating usually is not described by guides in rosy domestic terms, mama laying splendid tea tables for her little ones or mother bird rising early to get choice bits for her chicks. Instead, food delivery according to prenatal care guides more often sounds like military requisitioning. Doing the job well means thinking of food as fuel. Prenatal advice writers persistently avail metaphors of construction, demanding mothers provide building blocks for raising the baby's edifice. As much lies within her control, the mother is to provision the fetus properly. Failing to do so, she is warned, could damage her offspring for life.

Dieting is sometimes elected by pregnant women, though denounced by some writers concerned that maternal and fetal bodies both would lose necessary nutrients. Pregnant women have sometimes adopted restrictive diets under the conviction that a skinnier baby would be easier to deliver. It formerly was thought that babies would have softer bones if mothers limited intake of foods high in calcium and protein. Alice Bunker Stockham recounts favorably the experiment of a nineteenth-century man who removed the "earthy and bony matter" from his wife's prenatal diet and prioritized acidic fruit during pregnancy so the baby would have light bones and be easier to deliver. The boy born during this woman's untroubled labor was "finely proportioned and exceedingly soft, his bones resembling gristle. He became of large size and very graceful, athletic and strong as he grew up." Such a diet is unhealthy according to current understanding, but it does highlight perceived links between mother's eating and child's outcome. Pink in contrast warns that deprivation might harm the mother without achieving intended effect on the fetus, who could simply batten off of maternal stores: "Starvation of the unborn child is practically impossible, since the foetus has the power of living on his mother's reserves."[19]

Lore and science intuit that babies improperly provisioned can overcome the pregnant woman's mismanagement, to take what they need from her own stores of flesh and bone. Babies unhappy with what mothers serve even were thought to vote with their feet. Seventeenth-century theories suggested labor started when the fetus was not satisfied with the food provided in utero. Early modern writers feared that a woman could harm the fetus not just by eating too little but "surfeiting," effectively choking the child, either directly or indirectly by heaping up waste that would suffocate the fetus, "rendering [the blood] unfit to nourish the child or it fils [sic] the Vessels of the Womb which retain the child, ful[sic] of slime and snot."[20]

Overfeeding has been a grave concern on several fronts, especially in the present: flouting the equation of pregnancy and health, showing lack of discipline, and, perhaps most damnable, indicating selfishness in the woman's use of food rather than submitting to fetal good. Maternity guides from the early to mid-twentieth century demonstrate almost obsessive concern over the mother's weight. A mother's appearance matters to guide-writers. Ideals of female beauty in earlier centuries praised a wide-hipped, full-bellied look but concealed the obvious show of pregnant women. Fashions changed in the second half of the twentieth century, the "bump" put on display. Fashionable pregnancy now requires women to stay slim. Worrying that women could use side effects of pregnancy to justify overeating and weight gain, doctors and guide-writers removed that excuse. Writer Ellen Raymond reports that her doctor in 1951 put her on a diet to "make every pound count." A Catholic maternity guide placed rather ultimate judgment on pre-natal self-indulgence: "The modern emphasis on maintaining a good figure means a great deal also. . . . You may be excused some stoutness while carrying your baby, but you will be called to account after birth." This guide is hardly alone in turning consumption and weight gain into moral questions. Raymond accuses herself, regretting that when morning sickness lifted, "I suddenly developed a wanton urge to buy sweets and spices and starches," and she gains weight despite having "religiously" followed the diet her doctor advised.[21]

Pharmaceutical companies marketed and doctors prescribed appetite suppressants for pregnant women in the mid-twentieth century. Raymond declares her weight gain "alarming" by the seventh month though she had been faithfully taking her prescription diet pills, and at birth, justifies dieting as a necessity: "My diet turned out to have been not a convenience but a surgical necessity, for half the fifteen pounds I had gained proved to be baby. Dietary indulgence would have produced a child beyond my capacity to deliver normally." While obstetricians have become more permissive in the twenty-first century, Raymond's consciousness of the numbers—"the fifteen pounds"—reveals the way a woman's ideas about what is safe or healthy emerge from doctors' orders and load on moral freight. The long-running, bestselling pregnancy guide, *What to Expect When You're Expecting*, generated a stock of fresh phobias from the 1980s by itemizing the foodstuffs that a woman methodically must eat in order to provide adequately for the baby, while imposing a prim abstemiousness on the mother's own appetites. *What to Expect* bids pregnant women, before they put fork in mouth, to ask themselves whether this bite is the best they could give their babies. If they cannot answer in the affirmative, that fork should go right back down.[22]

Dietary guidelines for pregnant women assume that it is necessary to deliver the right supplies and that the woman might not know, by herself, what the baby needs. It is still not always obvious to mother or anyone else what the fetus wants or needs. The age-old puzzle of maternal cravings presented one way to address this mystery. Women when pregnant sometimes desire foods they ordinarily would dislike, dislike foods they ordinarily prefer, and sometimes feel these appetites intensely. Current pregnancy advice admits that there are actual physiological reasons for pica—the eating of dirt or chalk or metal because of dietary lack—but modernity mostly has defanged the power of cravings.

In earlier times the power of these appetites was taken more seriously. Denying them was thought to harm the woman or the baby. Folk tradition affirmed that a childbearing woman should be given what she craved, either because the craving somehow signaled that the work of growing the baby required that thing, or because the baby himself wanted that thing. In early modern Germany pregnant women caught stealing fruit were not prosecuted because pregnant women were thought to crave it, and were allowed. In a Catholic saints' lives account of the Blessed Thomas of Orvieto, a fourteenth-century Servite brother in central Italy, Thomas is honored for producing figs from a tree in winter in order to give them to pregnant woman who had a craving. A mother who craved strawberries during pregnancy but did not get them might birth a child with a red birthmark as evidence of the denial. Cravings could demonstrate the baby's request of a particular item or could impose cultural preferences on the fetus through things a woman ingested.[23]

The woman's work in safeguarding and supplying a baby should not be accounted merely instinctive or involuntary, but requires self-discipline and conscientious behavior for the good of the other. Even if a woman is given credit for providing the baby nutrients and nothing else—that ancient vision of woman supplying soil or matter to grow the creature a man generated—that provision must be recognized as an act that can be done well or poorly. Prenatal eating habits now help shape the whole experience of pregnancy, or even longer. Women in that period learn to consider the well-being of another human as immediately bound up with their own choices. That lesson is so powerful that for some it can even startle, after a baby is born and weaned, to find oneself eating and drinking for one's own good alone. But as nineteenth-century writer Prudence Saur reminds readers, "correct habits of diet and regimen are not the whole of right living." Saur maintains an unusually high view of gestational influence: women must not only offer the fetus nutritional building blocks but also the right emotions, "in harmony with the life forces of the universe." Protecting and provisioning can be difficult tasks. They point beyond the physical to higher attainments. Doing these tasks requires and fosters a kind of virtue.[24]

# 5

# *Pregnancy and the Practice of Virtues*

Pregnancy and childbirth have often been at least as perilous to women as battle has been to men—the prime arena for manly courage.

—Kayley Vernallis, "Of Courage Born" (2013)

If pregnancy and labor are to be understood as a "cross" which women must bear, all who witness the suffering of pregnant women should draw moral instruction from their example.

—Kathleen Crowther-Heyck,
"'Be Fruitful and Multiply'" (2002)

The gap between what a woman is expected to do during pregnancy and the guarantees she gets for doing it well leaves big questions open. Why is all this worth doing if it may not improve outcomes? How might the actions be evaluated as good? It may be safe to presume that a woman would want to aid her coming child, be inclined to do whatever necessary so that the child would be born healthy and well. This often is the case. But why and how she does these deeds matters too. Is it duty? A woman may be dutiful in following doctors' orders but usually has some higher motivation than that bringing her to the doctor's office in the first place. She could be acting out of an obligation to someone or something else, perhaps the coming child, a spouse, or her whole family. But here too obligation seems not the best way to explain her work of care. Treating pregnancy's work as obligation gives short shrift to a woman's choice in doing it and to the character of her behavior. It is a kind of gift. Duty and obligation fit imperfectly as tools to evaluate prenatal work. Looking only at outcome is not satisfactory either. A woman earnest in attending to prenatal care rules is doing more than doing no harm. Since the woman's doing well cannot necessarily guarantee results, testing her work against a standard of benefit or harm done to fetal outcomes is a poor measure.

More serviceable than these other measures might be an approach to childbearing informed by a view of virtue. Pregnancy encourages acts of care and recognition, acts that can be formative of character and not only of bodies. When a woman acts in these ways, she shows qualities admirable in human beings. Assessing courage in childbearing, philosopher Kayley Vernallis offers language that may apply generally to the virtues engaged in this phase of life. Starting, as such discussions do, with Aristotle, Vernallis defines virtues as "states of character," since "they tend, by their own nature, to the doing of the acts by which they are produced, and that they are in our power and voluntary, and act as the right rule prescribes." Virtue focuses attention on the person who acts rather than only evaluating actions themselves. Doing good acts shapes one into the kind of person who does good acts. Acting courageously makes one courageous. Courage may be easy to see in birth but may also be discerned throughout pregnancy, as Vernallis avers, "[w]e can more readily recognize and celebrate this form of bodily courage if we understand childbirth as a practice." Continuing to understand childbirth as a practice, a period of life shaped by a coherent set of actions oriented to the good of another, we may observe that pregnancy affords opportunity for the display and development of virtues.[1]

## Why Virtue?

The language of virtue belongs with the behaviors of pregnancy not least because the language of vice already tends to get assigned to pregnancy. In a telling expression, stressing the genetic basis of most disabilities by way of reassuring worried mothers, guidebook writers Drs. Oz and Roizen soothe, "The truth is, almost all of your vices will be forgiven." The agent of forgiveness in this system is neither the fetus nor some external authority but human helplessness before our own genes. This is cold comfort. Women are ordered to be scrupulous in their prenatal behavior as though it all matters *and at the same time* count this behavior futile because results are genetically predetermined. The self-creating baby can go on growing despite a woman's "vices" *but* the woman also must optimize the fetal environment.[2]

Describing some traits as "virtues" draws on an ethical tradition that roots human happiness in goods or ends specific to us as beings with reason. This tradition presupposes that human beings can reason about the good. In terms anatomized by Aristotle, adapted in Christian usage by Thomas Aquinas, and reinterpreted by many others, virtue is "an habitual and firm disposition to do the good." Theories about virtue carry long history and many subtleties, but here it is sufficient to emphasize that virtue attends not to isolated actions but to the character of the person doing them. Informed by reason, humans can practice acting well in a consistent way that develops habits of doing the good. In Aristotle's terms, "we become just by doing just actions, temperate by doing temperate actions, brave by doing brave actions." The good deed is not a one-off. Nor does a person, trained in virtue, need every single time to agonize over the right decision, or to force oneself to do right against one's own inclinations. Acting well may bring some kind of external reward but virtue, as the saying goes, is very much its own reward. The good is of a piece with the action, comes from within it rather than being pasted on as a bonus. Thus, being just or temperate is a good way to be, not just an instrumental path to getting some other prize. We learn virtue in part by observing others who already have it, moral exemplars, and by practicing it. Having virtue brings human flourishing.[3]

The seven virtues in traditional Western packaging include the four "classical" or "cardinal" ones esteemed among ancients in Greece and Rome—prudence, temperance, courage, and justice—plus the three "theological" virtues, faith, hope, and charity. The list is not exhaustive. Others, like hospitality, honesty, generosity, and patience, also can be named virtues. Virtue avoids error at extremes, the excess of a trait or the undersupply of it. For example, courage is the right intermediate state that falls between cowardice and rashness. Virtues are exhibited in the acts that a good person does, and other people learn to recognize virtues by watching those who show a good example. While some virtues may be harder to acquire than others, the good person need not—should not—strain but with practice act well and do so fluently.

Childbearing involves acting, not just passive waiting. The directives of prenatal care put priority on doing. What kinds of acts are involved, and how doing them can shape a woman, are appropriate to consider next. In some measure all seven virtues are called into service during childbearing. Hope, that bright hard way between despair and presumption, seems exactly the thing that women must keep when the process discourages and fetal outcomes are not guaranteed. Faith gives assurance of the unseen, the existence of the not-yet-visible child and his or her place in good creation. Temperance, the correct measure of enjoyment in pleasures of the flesh, might well describe the abstentions of the period. Justice, giving each his due, is rendered in providing the dependent fetus what is needed to come into life.

A few virtues are especially conspicuous in pregnancy. Prudence frames the whole as women discern and do the best for their own sake and on behalf of the expected child. Courage in the perilous passage of giving birth often has been compared to the battlefield bravery of men. Charity might be most obvious of all, as a woman gives because it is good for the child to exist. Hospitality makes physical and practical the gestures of charity. Actions taken on behalf of a fetus for nine months can shape habits, and the habits practiced come nine months closer to becoming permanent. A pregnant woman does not, say, only take vitamins once or twice or whenever she remembers or feels warmly disposed to a fetus in swallowing them. Instead, moving her behavior around the good of the coming child, she makes this practical step part of daily doings. One who has practiced behaving in a certain way for nine months can become a kind of person more nearly characterized by this generosity, attention, and care for another. The language of virtue helps us name the moral character of the work and take its example.

Strikingly, in her use of virtue language for discussing childbearing, Vernallis sets this approach *against* Christian tradition, charging Christianity with having "partially blinded us to the presence of courage in the practice of childbirth" by counting labor pain as a punishment for sexual sin, Eve's and our own, and by prizing chastity.[4] We may question Vernallis's approach to Christian moral teaching but recognize through it that religious belief is not prerequisite for viewing prenatal action in terms of virtue. Seeing pregnancy as a consciously shaped, coherent set of actions and choices makes virtue language appropriate to appraise this work. Through prudence, charity, hospitality, and courage a woman bears benefits to the fetus and nurtures good on her own part.

## Prudence

Prudence deserves first treatment among the virtues operative in pregnancy. Amid the classical virtues, prudence is primary, a leader for the others, discerning in practical terms what is right and how to do it. Aristotle calls prudence "a state, grasping truth, involving reason, concerned with action about things that are good or bad for a human being." Prudence, "this eye of the soul," refers not to mere caution or circumspection, as we tend now to take the term, but the reasoned exercise of sizing up what is and ordering behavior appropriately to follow. That former attribute is key. Prudence includes knowledge of universal principles in order to apply them rightly to particular situations, and the need for understanding conditions, the context and particulars of what is at hand, in order to anticipate their consequences.[5]

Appreciation of prudence sharpens the contrast between old, mistaken notions of reproduction and current presumably accurate ones. Prudence starts with seeing things as they actually are. If for millennia writers thought pregnancy was altogether something different and advised women to think the same, prudence requires that we begin to think better about it. We have got it wrong for so long. Now, getting it right, or what doctors now tell us is right, demands big shifts in thinking about what the body is doing. For the pregnant woman that might mean mapping onto her own belly a diagram of fetal development, then commanding her own action to eat, drink, seek medical care, avoid harm, and interpret symptoms. For others, onlookers, prudence dictates—this deserves repeating—an adequate grasp of reality, a true view of what is actually happening in childbearing. If science and medicine tell us that what is actually happening is that a woman's body is functioning specially to sustain her own strenuous labor and that of the growing fetus, onlookers should take note, and pay respect.

Rules may be universal, but the contingencies abundant in life require sensitive discernment in application. The pregnant woman confronts contingencies at every turn but with the added weight on her discernment, that her choices bear immediately and lastingly on somebody else. Prudence or practical wisdom begins with considering what is true, then judging what is to be done, and finally directing action accordingly. In all these respects, pregnancy engages prudence. It does so because prenatal care aims to shape how women *think* about pregnancy nearly as much as it shapes how they behave. Books for pregnant women assume that certain pieces of knowledge are appropriate and universally desired. How a fetus grows, how a woman's body might change, how to eat and exercise, which complications can be identified and avoided, what happens at medical appointments and delivery rooms—all find their place in books directed to the expectant mother. Sometimes guides add counsel on psychology, sex, work, or social situations. The books reflect general agreement about what women should want to know while pregnant.

But why? What is the purpose of knowing so much, thinking actively about pregnancy while pregnant? If the body is just going ahead on autopilot, the guts taking care of the bump, then it should not matter what is in a woman's head while the baby is growing. Concern over the pregnant woman's thoughts about pregnancy have a long history. Old notions suggested that the woman's thoughts, particularly her fears or aversions, could imprint the developing baby. While rejecting maternal impressions, some twentieth-century doctors believed that a woman's bad thoughts could make her nauseated, could wound or kill the baby. What women should think and not think both were targets for advice-givers' remediation.

The logic of prenatal care insists a pregnant woman should know a fair amount about her condition for a pair of reasons. First, she should know in order to behave appropriately. Knowing what the baby inside needs should prompt the mother-to-be to support those needs. Second, she should know in order to defeat worry. Pregnant women have been judged to cause grief by irrational fears, so turning away from fears should not only make things nicer for the mother but should positively improve health.

That first reason for knowing about pregnancy offers nearly a textbook illustration of prudence. Prudence is practical wisdom, assessing ways to act rightly based on right perception of reality. The woman is not only recognizing abstract facts about fetal development but observing how these scientific principles apply to her particular case. She translates fetal development information into practical usage, right reason in action. Understanding that a fetus needs calcium to build bones, for instance, a woman inspects her diet for adequate sources of the mineral and takes supplements if she discerns a need. Prudence consists in perceiving rightly what is, recognizing application of universal truth to particulars, and allowing such judgment to inform good action.

The second justification for informed motherhood, to avert worry, also requires prudence. Practical wisdom teaches right behavior between extremes of overreaction and the inability to act. Women now can know much more about fetal development and risk, but limits of that knowledge may increase women's fears without being able to allay them effectively. Pregnant women share worries that they might have harmed baby by standing too close to a microwave; listening to loud music; bathing in water too warm; eating deli meats, canned tuna, brie, or pineapple; drinking a champagne toast at a friend's wedding. But living must go on, and beyond a few obvious things it is hard to know exactly what will harm or help. Prudence engages the practical middle way between caring too little about prenatal disciplines and worrying too much.

### Charity and Generosity

Prudence may have a primary place among virtues in general but charity, love, is paramount among the virtues exercised in childbearing. Of course some pregnancies do not surge with the love of expectant parents to expected child. Still, in many pregnancies and certainly in social expectation of normal, wanted pregnancies, the woman's acts toward the child she carries are supposed to be motivated by charity. A definition of charity may start well with affirmation of the goodness of another's existence, in Josef Pieper's words, "It's good that you exist; it's good that you are in this world!" Allowing a fetus to be and offering nurture in the months before birth, a woman expresses this to the coming child: it is good that you are. Or in terms consistent with the prenatal period, because it is good, I will help you to be in this world.[6]

In his theology of the body, Pope John Paul II provides a way to think about how we love: love as a gift of the self. The body enables love as self-gift; we develop the self in order to have more to give. Pregnant women, through prenatal regimes of diet and discipline, work to acquire more to give. Prenatal care protocols in the United States sometimes treat these contributions as mandatory on a woman's part, fetal entitlement that comes with a mother's decision to carry to term. This social mandate should not obscure the fact that a woman's prenatal behaviors are given as a gift. The gift is not given stintingly. The goods of her body are laid before the fetus without limit. Structurally, the gestating woman makes all available and the child takes what she will. While the mother can choose which prenatal care strictures to obey or ignore, or find herself unable to follow all rules, it is not her prerogative to set bounds on what her body gives. By providing the fetus what is needed as best she understands it, the mother transforms the response to material need into gift rather than fetal appropriation. Her giving helps turn the takings of a stranger into a relationship with a loved one. A woman's giving in love to a fetus must not be reduced to instinct or to cartoon—mom giving herself because that's just what moms do, as in Virginia Woolf's biting caricature of maternal sacrifice, "If there was chicken, she took the leg; if there was a draught she sat in it"—but should be valued carefully.[7]

Charity in childbearing is exercised through the privations, accommodations, and deeds now customarily assigned pregnant women by doctors, instruction books, and the public at large. To some degree these codes of behavior do offer a training in temperance. That classical virtue prizes right responses to the pleasures of the appetites, finding and following a middle way between excess indulgence or denial. Temperance does resonate in prenatal care advisories. In an early twentieth-century guide published by the American Child Health Association, advisories come in exactly these terms, describing "the Expectant Mother" thus: "She lives simply. She eats nourishing food. She gets plenty of sleep, fresh air and mild exercise. She rests before she gets tired. She keeps herself cheerful and fit in every way." Prenatal motherly behavior might look like simple, clean living. Indeed, as critics of medically supervised birth sometimes charge, prenatal care can smack of social control, taking advantage of women's desires to have a healthy baby in order to squeeze their habits into bourgeois directions. Those criticisms can take an unnecessarily negative view of the process. The goal, after all, is to promote the health of offspring and woman alike, and a good diet and life habits do promote health better than does hard living.[8]

The virtue of temperance is of some help in describing prenatal practices. Temperance describes the reshaping of the appetites and not only the discipline of them, a temperate person learning to like broccoli and not just choke it down before dessert, with one portion of each pleasing more than two. But the classical virtue, temperance, may be less apt than the theological one, charity, to describe obedience to prenatal rules. The demands of charity can depart from temperance, requiring not a contented middle but something more nearly resembling a religious discipline. The penitential season of Lent, observed by many Christians in preparation for Easter, avails a better comparison for prenatal care. It is not an exact comparison. (And it is worth noting that pregnant and nursing women are exempt in Roman Catholicism from some Lenten rigors like fasting.) Still, the composite of prenatal care rules of abstention do bear likeness to an ascetic rather than temperate way. The idiom of prenatal instructions casts such codes in judgmental, even religious terms. Ellen Raymond reflects this tendency in her harsh words about the extra pounds she gained during pregnancy despite "adher[ing] carefully to my diet of pills and protein," despite "religiously" walking, despite going to bed when still "owing myself at least one of the four glasses of liquid allotted me each day," and despite battling her "wanton" cravings with a tape measure. It may be appropriate to reach for religious language to describe prenatal abstentions, though such language should be used carefully, avoiding the suggestion that this is any kind of redemptive sacrifice, or that it is the instinctual behavior of women alone. Or that it makes Everywoman like the one alone among her sex. Mary, as mother of Jesus, has been honored as a model for motherhood available to Christian women, but the singularity of her situation may make that model less than accessible to some women.[9]

Like Raymond, expectant women curtail superfluities—alcohol, tobacco, drugs, treats—to attend the better to others' necessities. Some mothers have to give not out of abundance but out of their own want. With calcium, for instance, if women do not provide enough through their consumption, the fetus can get what is needed by taking it from women's own stores, pulling from their own bones and teeth what is needed to build a body. Bernarr Mcfadden's maternity manual puts this calcium transfer in appropriately dramatic terms: "She is actually and literally sacrificed in order that her child may have, as nearly as possible, a fair start in life." The woman has to give the calcium, whether or not she has some to spare. To be sure, it is preferable that the mother consume calcium sufficient to provide for both her body and that of the fetus, but when that is not possible, the giving is zero-sum. She gives and fetus takes.[10]

Some ordinary habits or preferences a woman might give up because she chooses to or because they increase her own comfort during the period. But others she takes on because they are prescribed for those in her condition. Her privations are not directed to her improvement but the improvement of another. Her eating may become akin to fasting rather than temperance—but it is fasting on another's behalf. The mother's willingness to receive and obey prenatal counsel on such matters already reflects charity. Sometimes these abstentions, privations, and inconveniences are deemed helpful as preparation for motherhood. They may be that in moderate degree. Nevertheless, the charitable actions of pregnancy should be seen as moral acts in their own right rather than simply a dress rehearsal for infant care. The habits taken up by the pregnant woman are not significant only in making her a "mom," but in shaping the sort of person she is. The practice of watching one's consumption on behalf of another, of reckoning the impact of one's life on another's good, can be transformative in a thorough and lasting way.

While it is good that a woman's choices and abstentions actually benefit the fetus, a good is nurtured even in her wish to choose the better thing on behalf of the fetus. Observing protocols of prenatal care, women do not simply make decisions not to eat this or that, but take counsel from a medical professional. Some of the behavior doctors tell her to forswear might be bad in themselves, while others only harm in excess. The choice not to eat soft cheese because it might be infected with listeria (and therefore harm the fetus) or not to eat mackerel because it might contain high levels of mercury (and therefore harm the fetus), themselves *become* good works of a sort, done with an intent to benefit another and shaping the woman as the sort of person who considers the benefits of another when choosing. Directives to pregnant women often reflect risk assessments rather than conclusive proof, which is why such advisories have gotten pushback in recent years. Pregnancy presents opportunities to do well for another on best available knowledge. Even if not drinking that beer or not eating that brie does not absolutely prevent that particular fetus from harm, the woman's intent in abstaining nevertheless is to prevent harm.[11]

Abstinence in other pleasures of the flesh can seem nearly Lenten too. Sex during pregnancy has been controversial for centuries in maternity guides. Some early modern writers approved on grounds that, as the male seed gave the child form in the first place, continued exposure to seed would the more thoroughly impress the "stamp of the father" on the "shapeless mass" in the womb. Ecclesiastical disapproval of sex during pregnancy could be harsh, calling a husband making sexual advances to an expectant wife "a human monster." Writers from the late twentieth century are more likely to permit or encourage sex during pregnancy. Though a few earlier guides leave this matter blandly to private preference, a persistent emphasis through the mid-twentieth century strengthens justifications for avoidance. Medieval qualms about sex during pregnancy are not revived in these, but instead a combination of scientific guesses and sentiments support near total abstinence. A Catholic maternity guide from 1961 acknowledges that "[m]any ancient peoples believed it dangerous to engage in sexual relations during pregnancy" and therefore required abstinence, but declares that behaving considerately is sufficient rule.[12]

Some of these earlier prenatal care guides maintain that women should avoid intercourse for the first and last six weeks of pregnancy, plus during the time each month when they ordinarily would be having their periods. Some guides insist on prenatal celibacy for reasons vaguely spiritual. Others prefer abstinence out of respect for nature: "it is interesting to note that animals do not have any sexual intercourse during the period of pregnancy. The females are left alone by the males at this time as a matter of instinct, and we may be sure that this instinct has a sound and rational purpose." Often guides defer to the woman, their probable reader: if she feels like it she should go ahead, but if she does not, the couple should abstain from sex, a decision-making path that lends authoritative backing to a woman's request for avoidance. While conceding that "[t]here are many options as to the harm or desirability of sexual intercourse" and that any choice should "be carried on with great moderation," Josephine Baker gives the mother the choice, "and if the act is at all repugnant to her, or if it causes her any disturbance, either mental or physical, it should not be allowed to occur."[13] Most emphatic of all is Alice Bunker Stockham, whose esteem for "chastity during pregnancy" gives the woman a blanket exemption: "The mother should be exempt from the sexual relation during pregnancy." Stockham predicts that this gestational celibacy would make women "rejoice in a glad maternity, and a higher, nobler, and more God-like posterity will people the earth."[14]

## Charity in Sickness and Suffering

The charity essential to pregnancy may be most evident in the bodily discomfort the condition prompts. Parts of pregnancy feel like sickness. Indeed, for millennia the symptoms of pregnancy were practically synonymous with sickness, sickness the equivalent of a positive pregnancy test—"caught the disease," as one nineteenth-century woman writes of a friend. Or, in articulate 1950 terms, pregnancy starts "when you wake up with a nasty touch of the twenty-four-hour flu, and it ends some eight months later in the maternity wing of your friendly neighborhood hospital. . . . It's as welcome as the income tax." Not only nausea but aches, creaks, swelling, bleeding, and discombobulation are fully part of the experience, in different degrees universal to it. Pregnancy is not actual sickness but can feel like nine months' worth of being under the weather and also make women feel more susceptible to infirmity. Studying nineteenth-century Southern women, Anya Jabour observes that they "almost universally described pregnancy in terms of illness."[15]

In the mid-twentieth-century United States, prenatal care manuals reversed assumptions, pronouncing pregnancy a period of health rather than sickness. Construing pregnancy as healthy was a paradigm shift. Since many, including women themselves, have likened pregnancy to sickness, it took work for prenatal care advocates to rule instead that only very few pregnancies need be associated with misery and death, while most could be happy and comfortable if submitted to medical oversight. The healthy pregnancy is brought to you by the doctors' office; women were taught that they avoided being sick by becoming patients under maternity care.

Some women swear by healthy pregnancy, describing the nine months as normalcy, in part in order to oppose technological intervention. "What, then of the 'discomforts' or 'complaints' of pregnancy?" Barbara Katz Rothman asks in defense of a midwifery model of care, "The position that pregnancy is a healthy and entirely normal condition for mammals is of course politically necessary if midwives are to claim that they, as nonmedical people, are competent to attend to the needs of pregnant women." The position may be politically necessary and physiologically consistent but is inconsistent with many women's experiences, as Rothman concedes: "Being nauseated certainly does not *feel* healthy." Midwives address the problems by "minimizing these complaints" and addressing nutritional needs, assuring women the discomforts pass and are at base not a big deal.[16]

This becomes a different kind of distortion. Nevertheless, the idiom of pregnancy as a healthy and normal time fits awkwardly with women's actual experiences that feel far from her "normal." Dismissing discomforts of pregnancy is no more adequate a response to women's experience than the OB office solution of turning woman into a medical patient in order to avoid being sick. Being nauseated, fatigued, itchy, and swollen does not *feel* normal. Pains of childbearing come not only at the end. As Jesus acknowledges, the joy of a new child's birth makes women forget their travail (John 16:21), but the words that translators choose for what women feel in labor, words like sorrow, grief, anguish, or pain, show something irreducibly difficult about bringing a child into the world. Pursuing the space between these two approaches—sick to be healthy or health that feels like sickness—could yield a much better answer. The physical experience still demands explanation and not dismissal.

While some pregnant women choose obstetricians motivated by the promise of safer babies and deliveries, others come to it from a sense of unwellness. If OB visits are the place where feeling low and lousy in pregnancy gets taken seriously, the visits gain value for some women on those grounds. Attention to maybe-fragile female health during pregnancy is one way to ratify the importance of the experience. It is not an ideal way, but without alternative ways to process and affirm this experience, the prospect of having the "sickness" addressed, even sick-to-be-well sickness, can be a draw. A logic accompanies this embrace of pregnancy as a risky or sickly condition: given the size of the task, feeling put out by it feels about right.

Of pregnancy discomforts morning sickness is the most common. Morning sickness has troubled both women themselves and evangelists of ideals of healthy pregnancy. Plenty of women spend the first few months of someone else's life hunched over a toilet, or staving off dry heaves as they rise from bed in the morning. In the middle of the twentieth century, for some women who suffered "hyperemesis," or extreme vomiting during pregnancy, doctors prescribed thalidomide. The drug, never approved in the United States but used extensively in Europe, was prescribed to help reduce nausea. This remedy turned out to be worse than the problem, causing birth defects in the offspring of those who took the drug.[17]

But the fact that the feeling will pass, that it will get better at the fourth trimester if not the second, is not the point. In some ways made harder to recognize through cheerleading about healthy pregnancy, a woman's sick feeling is intimately linked with the fact of a new baby's being and health. Being pregnant presents dangers that women have to navigate carefully. Seventeenth-century physician Jacques Mauriceau likened a mother to "a good Pilot, who being imbarked on a rough Sea, and full of Rocks, shuns the Danger, if she steers with Prudence; if not 'tis by Chance if she [escapes] Shipwreck: So a Woman with Child is often in Danger of her Life, if she doth not her best Endeavor to shun and prevent many Accidents to which she is then subject." Inherent in pregnancy are demands on the body of the mother that expose her to dangers on behalf of her child. The likelihood of escaping final "shipwreck"—the norm for most American women by now, who anticipate bringing to term a desired baby in safe delivery—does not erase the dangers and discomforts throughout. While much pregnancy discomfort is occasioned indirectly by the growing fetus, other discomforts are utterly direct, if not quite intentional. With a fetus "kicking at her ribs, altering the shape of her body, shifting her bones from within," Lisa Guenther admits, the woman "bears the pain of the Other *for the sake of the other.*"[18]

Nausea and swelling ankles are evidence of charity exercised in carrying a baby. Every woman carrying a baby gives costly gifts, but some pregnant women make this more evident than others. Bringing into the world a new human being gives you hemorrhoids. Some helpful interpretive scheme ought to exist to make sense of this fact, something more precise than the fall or an evolutionary wrong turn. Instead of resolving this puzzle of pregnancy, in popular culture errors commonly are made in a few different directions. One error is to feel bad about feeling unpleasant: women might gripe but feel guilty about doing so, as if admitting to an upset stomach was a sign that they did not love their babies enough. This error was given a perverse sort of approval by some in the medical profession in the middle of the twentieth century. It may seem implausible that any woman would choose nausea but some doctors argued this. As they observed cases of morning sickness that persisted in spite of medical pronouncements that decreed pregnancy happy and healthy, some physicians and psychiatrists theorized that these women really might be wishing their babies away. Doctors interpreted nausea as a kind of rebellion against pregnancy. For Cyril Pink, not going quite this far, courage could manage morning sickness. While it is "unquestionably a depressing business to feel sick and feeble all day," the best women "carry on just as usual in a really marvellous way," simply excusing themselves "several times an hour to be sick," demonstrating there a "courageous attitude." [19]

Another error in interpreting the havoc pregnancy wreaks is to make light of the unpleasantness. Often the discomforts get painted with humor, rued in girlfriend guides as the kind of freaky side effects that just happen on the way to motherhood. Some of the process is funny, sure, but by itself the laugh-track version of pregnancy is as inadequate as the attribution of all to hormones or the holistic claims that nausea is healthy and normal. A better way to explain that pregnancy is both a normal work of the body and can feel downright wretched is to emphasize the significance of the work. The woman, doing something normal and healthy, is also accomplishing something worthwhile and difficult for another person's particular good and for human flourishing in general. Who we are as human beings is found in this, that it actually is the case that bringing a new person into the world gives someone else hemorrhoids or heartburn, tears and scars. Evolutionary biologists may explain that the danger of labor is owing to humans' colossal brain, that what endangers a mother is matching her little pelvis with that big head. Likely it is not passing along a big brain that pregnant women credit most in explaining their willingness to undergo the whole ordeal. Love underlies willingness to bear this infirmity on behalf of another's becoming.

For some women the body proclaims this truth right in the midst of gestation: the pregnant body is literally going to seed. The romanticizing of healthy pregnancy makes this discombobulation harder to admit, as does decades' worth of starlets flaunting bumps but otherwise showing the camera their own unchanged spectacular selves. Maternity manuals have been selling the prospect of glamorous pregnancy for decades. Ordinary women observing these images in magazines or on screens may simultaneously resent and admire such pictures, images that contradict beholders' experience of what pregnancy is like. "Having a baby can be simple," *Modeling for Motherhood* concludes, "Recovery can be easy. You can keep your charm, improve your health . . . and afterwards get your figure back, slim and smooth as ever. Maybe slimmer and smoother!"[20]

For other women infirmity becomes more apparent after pregnancy is over. Humans' energies are spent in the effort to engender their replacements. We are like most other creatures in this respect. The worn-out features of some women's old age are not only evidence of time but traces left behind from giving life. Women wear that evidence on the body after pregnancy in varicose veins, wide flattened feet, mottled skin, thinned hair, droopy breasts, and stretch marks. The husk is left with traces of the fruit borne ripe. And these signs following normal births are mild compared to the evidence left behind from deliveries gone awry. In places with ample medical resources tears get repaired, but scarring and fistula are devastating to women—particularly in parts of Asia and sub-Saharan Africa—where the wounds of childbirth render them social outcasts.[21]

Having babies depletes their bearers. That is not an argument against having babies. Serums, vitamins, yoga classes, and plastic surgery are marketed to hide the evidence, but hiding the evidence only impedes recognition of what actually is going on in childbearing. Offering oneself in the service of another is the charity women offer to their children, to the ongoing course of human life on earth. That charity should be recognized whether women retain or erase the spots, marks, and scars of the experience. Pregnancy is practical willingness to be spent in the service of another's good, in the present months and thereafter.

Not seldom, illness in pregnancy presents women with difficult choices. The unusual situation of living in a body with another person makes problems in case of maternal illness. Sometimes mother and baby share the damage. For some ailments, maternal systems shield the fetus from serious harm. Still other maladies can leave the fetus unharmed but be potentially deadly to the mother. Mothers with preexisting conditions, asthma or diabetes or epilepsy or heart trouble, may be in extra danger during pregnancy or be unable to pursue usual means of treatment lest these hurt the fetus.

Mothers' "sickness" is not supposed to be unto death. No one dies in childbirth any more—although actually they do, even in developed countries, and in tragic numbers in places with more poverty and less medical care. Studies in the United States in 2017 revealed disturbing rates of maternal mortality, 17.3 per 100,000 live births, a count some estimate as too low but still the highest among affluent countries. Researchers judge the majority of these deaths preventable, resulting from medical professionals' failure to diagnose conditions like eclampsia or hemorrhage, and from tendency to focus more on infant than on mother. In the past, the higher likelihood of death or disfigurement during pregnancy or delivery was a recognized part of the experience of motherhood. Historian Judith Walzer Leavitt observes that childbearing women fell "under the shadow of maternity," carrying the "seeds of their own destruction" and requiring preparation for death since "a possible death sentence came with every pregnancy." In his staggering study of the subject, *Death in Childbirth,* Irvine Loudon gives credit to antiseptics and antibiotics for the healthy survivable births we take for granted. There is nothing quite like the loss of a mother in childbirth, the extinguishing of one life at the arrival of another. For a woman whose survival is compromised by pregnancy, the choice may come to take one life over the other. Choosing the child's survival over one's own is not an act to be taken for granted, but is an extraordinary choice and a potentially heroic one.[22]

Gianna Beretta Molla offers an example of one making such a choice. Born near Milan in 1922, Molla was a devoted Catholic woman who studied medicine and became a respected physician, predominantly serving women, children, and the poor. After marrying Pietro Molla, she had three children, along with a pair of miscarriages, and continued her medical practice. In her sixth pregnancy Molla developed a uterine fibroma. More extensive treatment for this tumor could have come through hysterectomy or abortion. Molla instead chose limited treatment, having only the tumor removed. She then carried the pregnancy to term, with pain. A week after the birth of her healthy daughter, thirty-nine-year-old Molla died. Beatified in 1994 and canonized in 2004 by Pope John Paul II, Molla was the first married laywoman to be named a saint and, Vatican watchers note, also the first "working mom" to be canonized. The pope described Molla's childbirth as a "conscious immolation." Ceding her own survival in order to protect her daughter's, Molla exercised extraordinary virtue, voluntarily and beyond the requirement of Catholic moral theology. By report of the physician's family, radical self-gift already was an ordinary part of her life and work.[23]

It is one of the singular blessings of our time and place that stories of death in childbirth, though yet persistent, are rare. Those occasions are extreme examples of the charitable self-sacrifice more common to ordinary pregnancy. Molla's "conscious immolation" is extraordinary in degree rather than in kind. To be pregnant is to open oneself to the prospect of great pain, to accept a condition that can feel unpleasant or agonizing or can require embrace of great loss. Part of the experience of pregnancy is the ongoing possibility that things could go badly wrong, that miscarriage, stillbirth, fetal distress, or perilous labor could occur. The pregnant woman walks through this whether or not the worst actually happens in her particular pregnancy.

## Hospitality

The hospitable character of pregnancy not only is prerequisite for each individual life but provides the precondition for human life and social connection more generally. As all human life starts from the body of another, "woman's pregnant flesh," Frances Gray argues, is "the original home and ground of human sociality." A childbearing woman displays not only the telltale signs of a new person-to-be but a sign of human receptivity to relationship. Only because each one of us was first accommodated do we have capacity to care for ourselves or extend generosity to others.[24]

Pregnant women offer the developing fetus a protected space to stay for a while, ample share of whatever is at table, bed and board. The comparison likening pregnancy to hospitality may be a little overused. Taking the common metaphor, for instance, Nicholson Eastman quips that menstruation is like "the breakdown of a bed which was not needed because the 'boarder' did not materialize." But the parallels between pregnancy and hosting a houseguest are irresistible—and illuminating. When a guest comes to stay in our home, we might move furniture, prepare a room or couch, change linens, adjust our plans around guests' needs, offer special meals, give welcome. A pregnant woman does all of those things inside the space of her own body. The woman "has no extra room to give to the child," but in Lisa Guenther's nice phrase, "contracts to make space for the Other within itself." The fetus moves in. The pregnant woman accepts discomforts caused by the guest. Her internal furniture, organs, muscles, bones, are moved around to make space for the growing resident. Paradoxically she becomes smaller even as she looks bigger, her organs drawn into restricted space to make space for the temporary resident. In naming pregnancy as a kind of "original hospitality" or "radical hospitality," some feminist scholars have shown further dimensions of this familiar metaphor, the woman's hospitality in her body the source of all others. The woman does not merely "make room," that is, move over to share space. She *makes* the room where it was not before, taking on new dimensions in order that the fetus have it.[25]

The mother gives the fetus a place to live on the earth. Regrettably, this maternal function sometimes gets construed the wrong way as *merely* shelter. Misused in the past, the metaphor of pregnancy as hospitality deserves to be reclaimed. Ancient images of woman as soil or nest, or modern imagination of the whole woman as the shell of the fetal apartment, err in characterizing this work as involuntary. James Mumford recognizes the metaphor of mother-as-container is "misleading," because the relationship between woman and fetus is a "coexistence." The pregnant woman does not just offer the body surrounding the fetus inside, but actively offers to supply the needs of the "newone."[26]

Pregnant women may or may not have extended a particular boarder an invitation. Sometimes pregnancies are energetically sought out, the boarder avidly recruited. But one has literally no idea whom the boarder will be, who will come to take up a startlingly intimate space. Sometimes prospective parents have a clearer idea of whom they are inviting in. Biological mother and father might envision someone like a blend of themselves, at least a blend of the most loved elements of themselves. Parents might have a clearer picture still when assisted fertility technology has allowed choice of an embryo that has certain characteristics. Still, many women never extend explicit invitation yet ably accommodate the unexpected guest. Simply allowing the fetus to stay, and then actively taking care of him or her while present, constitutes a generous permission. Even in the most wanted pregnancy, even in an uncomplicated one, this permission is never a small thing.

Estimating the hospitality of pregnancy, one might contend that care for the fetus can be selfish, even a kind of self-care. Stingingly Søren Kierkegaard makes this claim: "For as a wife, as mother—whew! It is an egotism which man has no inkling of. . . . it is the most violent egotism, in which I daresay she does not first love herself, but through 'egotistically' loving what is hers, she loves herself."[27] Love for the coming child here is construed simply as love for something identified as one's own, attachment for something claimed as "mine," or else a self-interested desire to put out the best "product" since a healthy baby is an easier outcome for the mother herself.[28] Alternatively, one might protest that the child is no stranger at all. Tradition, after all, insisted on the familiarity of the being harbored by the woman, since its origin was the child's father—presumably a person plenty familiar to an expectant mother. A fetus thought to spring from the father's seed is emphatically not a stranger (or a stranger's child!) but a bit of its male parent.

The way we now understand the genetic composition of the fetus instead highlights the strangeness of the new-forming body temporarily housed. The child is not simply extra flesh on the mother nor implanted remnant of the father but someone else. The new creature is a being no one ever has met before. The fetus arrives at an hour the woman does not expect. Even in planned pregnancies, the woman whose body becomes residence cannot be exactly sure when the embryo began. Gray observes that the hospitality of pregnancy is not extended to a "preexisting guest," but as "an actualizing of being, an enabling of life that has not previously existed." The guest comes into being through the hospitality. The embryo unfolds as an unknown person. As the narrator of Lionel Shriver's novel *We Need to Talk about Kevin* admits after sex, "It's very dangerous. . . . Indeed just about any stranger could have turned up nine months later. We might as well have left the door unlocked." Sentimentality sometimes encourages expectant parents to deny this risk, to ascribe dearness or their own personalities to the unknown child-to-be. Parenthood commonly unmoors those pretenses. Parents again and again discover their children to be strangers.[29]

James Mumford reminds that even "the most planned of pregnancies" also can be "the most contingent of encounters," since "what there will never be control over is the 'who' of the one conceived. That a couple want a 'baby' is one thing; that they get Marcus is something quite different, outside all their imaginings and beyond their expectation." Even as parents believe God makes the child, or that God has given them their particular child as a blend of their own united love, they confront a child whose identity is yet to be revealed. Pregnancy is an ongoing act of welcoming the stranger even as that hospitality transforms the stranger into a beloved person. Every person who comes to be does so because a woman provided this hospitality.[30]

Scripture and the early church alike enjoined hospitality as an important duty of the faithful. Kindness to strangers could turn out to be entertaining angels unaware, or offering welcome to the Lord himself (Matt. 25:35; Heb. 13:2). Benedict of Nursia, the central Italian founder of a religious order and rule-shaping monastic practices from the sixth century through our own time, instructs monks to receive visitors with the head bowed and the body prostrated as though receiving Christ in the person of the guests. Dorothy Day's biographer reports that, for the founder of the Catholic Worker movement, the birth of a daughter initiated her "ministry of hospitality," as it "all began with the hospitality of the womb." The hospitality of childbearing requires not only simple self-abnegation, a bowing out of the way to favor another, but an active, continual giving in which the woman simultaneously offers herself and aids the child.[31]

The pregnant woman is an instructive model of generosity. As a generous host will provide for a houseguest, a mother gives the fetus the best she has to offer. On rare occasions the space might be amiss. The woman sometimes cannot give the guest all she would wish because she has so little herself. Even among the very poor the fetus has a luxurious bed, accommodated in utero in more comfort, abundance, and safety than ever might be experienced—for those of uncertain means—after birth. For some children, the room in the womb might be the best place they ever live. The residence the woman provides for the fetus is, most of the time, exactly the right kind of room, right size, shape, temperature, including both closet and wastebasket. Human beings provide the best shelter for each other at the fragile, vulnerable beginning of life.

Frances Gray's reservations in the case of an unwanted pregnancy perhaps inadvertently underscore the abundance of this hospitality. Having described pregnancy as radical hospitality, Gray likens an unwanted fetus to sparrows who nest in the roof of one's house. Gray weighs options by which a woman may decide to allow the sparrows, messy and boisterous, to stay, but emphasizes that a woman is not obligated to do so: "it is not incumbent on every woman to either exhibit or to maintain absolute hospitality in every circumstance." Gray's argument for evicting the sparrows, that "they wake me early, make a mess everywhere, and are taking over the place," is serviceable as an illustration for the trouble a fetus can produce. The metaphor errs, though, in its estimate of the relationship between the fetus and the woman. The fetus is not like a sparrow, an unbidden squatter borrowing space in a place where it does not belong, but is intrinsically *like* the mother, generated originally and continually from the woman's action and her own stuff, genetic and nutritive. The fetus is a stranger but not altogether strange to her. From awareness that a reproductive act could engender a child, to recognition that conception has occurred, to daily doings to enable one's body to support the fetus, the woman cooperates in generating and cultivating the stranger she hosts.[32]

Pregnancy embodies community. It requires life together, not just in proximity with another but under the skin. The continuation of human life depends on the partial sacrifice of autonomy that women make in childbearing. Learning to extend oneself on behalf of the child in utero and observing women who provide this aid and comfort help to nurture community within and beyond the family. Recognizing prenatal hospitality can help onlookers grow in their capacities too. It is not only mothers who should behave responsibly for others but all, because we all have been borne and do not come to be by ourselves. The gift of birth, Lisa Guenther argues, "implicates me in responsibility for a stranger whom I have not yet met, but to whom I am already bound to give welcome."[33]

## Courage

If charity is the virtue most evident during childbearing, courage just as obviously is the one prioritized in birth. Plutarch recorded that the graves of women who died in childbirth, like men who died in battle, were honorably marked because they signified a sacrifice important to the larger community. The comparison might have been more popular before antiseptics and antibiotics made birth safer and anesthesia made it less painful. Indeed the need for courage when entering hospital labor-and-delivery suites now may seem muted. Still, it is a significant aspect of the experience. Childbirth education teaches ways to manage fear as much as those to manage pain. Some, including the Lamaze and Bradley methods, suggest that putting fear aside helps reduce pain and facilitate birth.[34]

Courage traditionally was credited to birthing women, and Kayley Vernallis sees reason for renewed emphasis on courage in birth. Marking courage in childbearing need not be lost, either, because many women do birth in ways less dangerous or painful than in some past situations. Women appropriately rebuff assumptions that delivery needs to be natural, that is, without pain relief, in order for them to be validated as good mothers. Labor without pain relief is not what makes childbearing an act marked by courage. Instead, openness to danger and the unpredictable needs of a child thread that virtue through the nine months and beyond them.[35]

Bearing and birthing a child not only engage a private willingness to suffer pain on behalf of a (to-be) loved one, but what Vernallis calls physical pro-social courage. The classical conception of the virtue attributed this courage only to men, while the corresponding virtue in women was classed as something private and instinctual. To the contrary, Vernallis insists the courage women exhibit in childbearing is just as much oriented to the common good. It is not involuntary. It requires her bold willingness to bear harm, even her own death. Like a soldier in battle or a firefighter entering a burning building, the childbearing woman confronts serious risks in service of a larger good, willingness even to die in service of that good. This willingness gets us to the heart of the weight borne by women in pregnancy. Women confront mortality—their own, their children's—and death as a fact of human life. To do so they exercise both physical strength and a kind of mental self-mastery to persist through the hardship to the end.[36]

Since this, like all virtues, describes a habit rather than a single action, an aspect of character shaped by practice of choosing and behaving in service of the good, we note that courage is engaged not only in labor but throughout pregnancy. The courage of childbearing comes long before the first contraction. Women exercise courage as they open themselves to the bodily afflictions of bringing forth life. Courage comes in hard cases, when pregnancy may expose a woman to harm, require her to entrust her child to others, or make a choice between her own life and the child's. Women bear beloved children forth to a world where others may not always meet them with love—even those most close. We may take a lesson from the sand tiger shark, whose babies sometimes eat each other in utero. Shark mothers may remain in blessed ignorance, but not human mothers. The first son born to Eve, whom Genesis names the mother of all of living, turns out to be the death of her second (Gen. 3:20, 4:1–8). Generations later when Rebekah, mother of Jacob and Esau, finally gets pregnant, her belly roils with the combat of her twins and she cries out to God, "Why is this happening to me?" (Gen 26:22–23) While most human mothers may be spared the experience of sibling rivalry from under the skin, few if any are spared the grief of beholding hostilities shared by humans carried in the same womb.

Being pregnant includes the possibility of bearing not a living child but one who does not live, literally bearing death in one's own living body. Consider the courage of a woman whose conscientious prenatal observance ends with a stillbirth. "There is no other experience, in the mix of our many human griefs, that comes close to mirroring this," L. Serene Jones ponders about the woman who miscarries or delivers a stillbirth. "She carries death within her body . . . but she does not die," but instead this woman becomes "the self who is meant to produce, be creative, give life, and make a future, but who rather holds the stench of decay in the depths of her being."[37]

Courage is also needed for those who bear children whose lives will be shaped by disability or unusual suffering. Recognizing need for courage, a Catholic maternity guide offers women reassurance on grounds that the odds were "overwhelming" that a baby would be normal, though "the odds are also heavily against your having a 'perfect baby,'" and "every parent faces the possibility that the infant may not measure up mentally." The writer of this Catholic guide assures parents that they should be "prepared to accept any child which God in His Divine Wisdom gives them," a preparation that surely takes courage. That courage of childbearing is not a momentary confrontation of pain at delivery but a virtue sustained over long periods of care in time of danger.[38]

The courage exercised in childbearing has been muted not only by improvements in obstetric medicine, but by overemphasis on its instinctual or natural character. Some pioneers of the natural childbirth movement advocated labor without drugs not as a heroic act but on grounds that women, without unnecessary fear, would be able to reclaim the apparently painless childbirth experienced by primitive women. This approach paid civilized, white women the flattery of blaming their pain on their advanced good manners, while denying possibility of courage to them or their "primitive" sisters.[39]

It can be desirable to minimize or manage labor pain through natural means, but a mistake to behave as though pain is outside the process. In Japan, Vernallis notes, women are expected to go through labor without medication. But it is not idealized as a peaceful process but an arena of fierce perseverance and courage. Custom there instructs women to labor without crying in order to demonstrate strength, mas-

tery over suffering, composure, courage. Susan Windley-Daoust recommends a different approach, fearless strength shown not as soldier-
ing on but "giving place" or "yielding" to God and to the baby's passage
out. The good here is not the pain itself but the courage engaged in
birth, whether excruciating or less so.[40]

Just as morning sickness and swollen ankles do not discount the
charity of pregnancy but make it all the more obvious, pain of labor may
underscore the courage of the act. When obstetric anesthesia first became practicable in the middle of the nineteenth century, its defenders
had to answer criticism that they were thereby robbing women of some
spiritual good in childbirth. The argument made by some that taking
pain out of labor impiously denied Eve's curse was pretty handily put
away. But anesthesia resistors were not wrong to intuit that something
spiritual might inhere in the pain of labor. A twentieth-century obstetric anesthesiologist was crestfallen to discover that "many women did
not want my help," in part because pain was among the features of birth
that showed its significance.[41]

Even when a woman receives an epidural, pain remains a part of
birth. In her assessment of the courage of birth, Margaret Hammer takes
meaning from the fact that, as Jesus defeated death by going through it,
birth draws women through the threat of death for another to be born.
Preachers in previous centuries took perhaps too much advantage of labor's dangers to exhort women to repentance and piety. The possibility,
as New England Puritan minister Cotton Mather put it, that a woman's
childbed linen would be her winding sheet, renders pregnancy a time
to reckon with mortality. It is progress of large proportions that most
women in developed countries no longer have this expectation of their
childbed sheets. Lower probability of imminent death does not mean
the event is no longer momentous nor ineligible for courage.[42]

While medicalized childbirth can mute the deadly perils of delivering new life, it may paradoxically heighten the need for courage *before* delivery. Unlike mothers in earlier times and places, expectant mothers under sophisticated medical care are held responsible not only for keeping the baby in and getting the baby out, but for navigating the obstacle course of dangers that ordinary life presents to women conscious of their perils. Prenatal care offers increased safety but at the same time may require more courage as women struggle to evaluate each action they take in light of fetal prospects. Some women must take courage in going ahead with a pregnancy when its continuation is difficult. Living out a decision to bear a child to term—especially a child unplanned or unwell—calls for courage as the bearer works on behalf of the coming child, even as the work exposes her to suffering.

In many times and places pregnant women were not to walk about in public because their very shape made too plain things deemed best hidden—sexual experience, bodily changes. Modesty presupposed preference for concealing the details of human emergence. Now, women walking about big-bellied in broad daylight provide models, of sorts, of prudence, charity, hospitality, and courage. This need not be read reductively, as though women must be or just naturally are more disposed to feminine self-sacrifice. Instead observers might be reminded again of what it took for them, for each of us, to come to be. We know that a long investment of time, a pathway of practical disciplines and self-abasements, are asked on behalf of each person coming newly into the world. Virtue is fostered by moral exemplars. We can take the lesson.

To be sure, not every woman will think of every pregnancy this way. Still, in the cultivation of virtue it is helpful to see what virtue looks like: How does a generous person behave? How does a brave person behave? What shows charity? Moral exemplars or role models help others learn what it looks like to live well. Thinking about pregnancy this way helps onlookers to see in a pregnant woman a kind of example. For if a woman's positive acts on behalf of the fetus accomplish some goods internally, for the child and for herself, those acts can accomplish goods on the outside as well as they provide a model and a reminder. A pregnant woman is able to know what the fetus is doing in the body, what she may or should do to facilitate it doing well. She is able to apply what she knows in general, how fetal development works, to the particular situation in which she finds herself with child. That is her exercise of prudence. For those around her the cogitation might go in the reverse direction. Observing a particular woman's doing reminds us how human beings come to be, and recognizing again the consistent giving, generosity, courage of the pregnant woman can present a model of what those things look like elsewhere.

# 6

# *Pregnancy in Identity and Relationship*

[T]he fundamental dimension of man's existence is a co-existence.

—Pope John Paul II, *Crossing the Threshold of Hope* (1994)

The baby is begotten by two but brought forth by one.

—James Mumford, *Ethics at the Beginning of Life* (2013)

I am not myself today," people sometimes say to excuse themselves when feeling unwell or behaving uncharacteristically. Pregnancy is a period when a healthy woman might avail herself of this explanation. She is not exactly herself. She is in some ways both less and more than herself. Inasmuch as we draw the borders of a person approximately around her skin, the pregnant body encloses not only the woman's self but the self of someone else.

Pregnancy's disciplines and habits of mind can resonate long after the due date has passed. Prenatal attentiveness to the body—one's own and one's imagination of the fetus—can bring about differences in one's behavior thereafter. Even after the baby is delivered, a woman might understand herself differently inside. Outside, that experience of expecting can shift how others see the woman and find themselves in relationship to her. Thus in identity and relationship both, the effects of carrying life may make changes.

A pregnant woman is a strange person, strange to herself and others, as her shape and thoughts blur and distend, as she generates desires and disgusts foreign to her settled preferences. During her life before and after pregnancy, she eats, exercises, dresses as she chooses (and/ or as appropriate to the time and place she inhabits). But during this period she may be less than ordinarily able to determine the sort of self she presents to the world. She may be, temporarily, less distinguished for other accomplishments, more defined by the milestones of gestation. The double-bodied character of pregnancy is weird not because it is rare but because it is at once utterly ordinary *and* starkly unlike the experience of the human adult when not pregnant. A pregnant woman is (at least) two-headed and eight-limbed, with parts of her own body out of her control, unable to control the other body inside hers that kicks, rolls, nudges. Having more than her own self in her body, a woman self-consciously maintains a temporary condition both normal and bizarre, awaiting another new status. Pregnancy makes a woman appear in some respects more herself, aware of being shaped by her history, family, and embodiment. She also is in some respects more than herself, greater than usual in shape and sometimes even in habits of good character, containing another person and that person's future.[1]

Hers can be strangeness in a good way. After all, much of the logic of prenatal care comes down to a self-improvement project configured to making the self more able to sustain someone else. A woman is not just giving of herself for another's good, she is giving the coming stranger a better version of herself. The language of self-gift from Pope John Paul II in his *Theology of the Body* bids humans to nurture virtue in themselves so that they might more generously give in relationships. To the epigraph quoted above, that the fundamental dimension of our existence is coexistence, Susan Windley-Daoust adds, "the woman carrying a child in her womb could not be a more radical representation of that insight." The now-canonized pope may not have had the maternal-fetal relationship primarily in focus. But his idea helps put in the most positive light what the prenatal regime could be about. Prenatal practices are not best understood in medical-obedience terms or in zero-sum terms. Instead prenatal care could be cast in terms of abundance, making more of you to have more to give to the other.[2]

A pregnant woman is encouraged to keep herself in good health to sustain systems that sustain a fetus. The fetal development habit of mind encouraged by prenatal care reminds the pregnant woman that her labor is constantly required by this project, whatever other work falls to her hands. Even when a woman is not credited with consciously producing the infant, her organs are praised for chugging along to bring the desired good. While the conscious work of childbearing is considerable, the involuntary functions are impressive on their own. Since these systems lie hidden below the surface, these capacities can startle mother and beholder alike. What the female body does in switching from nonpregnant to pregnant condition is fully amazing, systemically so. The bump, that symbol of maternity made cute, is not the point. Much more impressive than the rounded belly are whole systems of the body repurposed from one mode to another. Organs get mobilized into a bewildering range of duties. The woman does not consciously make all this happen. Indeed, inability to consciously control the process can be one of the great frustrations of human life, whether in cases of infertility or in unintended pregnancy.

Pregnancy can shift self-understanding of the body in varied ways. Some of these ways are conspicuous, involving the sexed character of the body. Some of these are subtle, involving microscopic elements that we take on faith as constituent parts determining who we are and what we have to do with others. And some of these changes must be considered not in isolation but as they connect a woman to others before her and around her.

Gender equality, even in the breach, encourages American women in many spheres to consider femaleness less than relevant to what they do. But in childbearing, femaleness gets emphasized bluntly and persistently. Female parts, having new names, get sequestered for their reproductive functions. Nipples are for nursing; the birth canal is for birthing. Pregnancy's reinterpretation of femaleness is complex, in language and experience, sometimes emphasizing sexuality, sometimes casting the individual woman as cog in the wheel of species continuation. This invitation to reconsider what one is can be startling, especially as some women otherwise walk around giving little thought to the uterus or its attendant apparatus in life. Further, the novel doings of the body can seem at odds with the workings of the mind. Western tradition has sometimes set them at odds, especially for females, an inheritance from Plato that Cynthia D. Coe claims with ambivalence: "this dualistic idea that one may be pregnant *either* in body or in mind, but not both." Women philosophers have written provocatively of their ability to hold the two together, as in Iris Marion Young's positive account of being simultaneously absorbed in the movements of mind and body:

> I walk through the library stacks searching for the *Critique of Dialectical Reason*; I feel the painless pull of false contractions in my back. I put my hand to my belly and notice its hardening, while my eyes continue their scanning. . . . In attending to my pregnant body in such circumstances, I do not feel myself alienated from it, as in illness. I merely notice its borders and rumblings with interest, sometimes with pleasure, and this aesthetic interest does not divert me from my business.

But others, onlookers, bystanders, may not credit this. Coe reports one student judging her unfavorably, offering in course evaluations, "It didn't help that she was pregnant. Hormonal."[3]

### Physical Changes from Carrying on the Lineage

From the moment of pregnancy diagnosis, features of prenatal care culture invite a woman to think differently about who she is, even what she calls herself. She might have been accustomed to name particular parts of her body in a certain way—flat (or flabby) stomach, a flat (or buxom) chest, thin (or mighty) thighs—but is assigned new terms to describe and assess them. Virtually no part, however seemingly unrelated to gestation, gets left out of resultant transformation. Hair thickens, thins, or curls; the nose catches odors more keenly; toes may appear lost over the abdominal horizon and feet may grow longer and wider. Learning to name one's body parts according to the doctor's terminology is a way of obeying conventions of pregnancy, of claiming membership in a group by using its jargon. The unique individual might become at once less recognizable to herself—why is my hair doing this?—and more generically identifiable as a maternity patient.

Marks right on the skin make pregnant women identifiable as such. Some expectant women get an indefinite "bloom," a glow that signifies its own kind of beauty between the nubile and the matronly. Some markings may be challenging to count as improvements. Pregnancy can cause darkening spots here and there on the face. Women are reassured that this pigmentation, called chloasma, is normal due to elevated estrogen and melanin levels. The popular nickname for chloasma is the "mask of pregnancy," suggestive of a temporary facade cast over a woman's own usual face to signal her change of estate. Even the marks' temporary status is significant, a sign that the woman looks like a different person on the outside because she is different inside in her person, holding a different person in her insides.[4]

In addition to spots dotting her face, other short-term markings may be invisible to passersby. The most noteworthy new mark is the linea nigra, highlighting reproductively relevant body parts, line from navel to pudenda, dividing the woman in two. The line both connects and splits. Connects: ancestry and posterity are points on a continuum, from the navel recalling her origins to the place where descendants enter the world. Splits: the line is like a positive pregnancy test written right on the body itself. Pregnancy draws a line between before and after, the body on its own versus the body shared with someone else.

As experiential reality, what goes on in the pregnant gut, its cravings and food aversions, make more sense as puzzles of identity than just of nutrition, which is the way they customarily are handled by advice manuals. While no one besides the woman herself can attest that she once liked bacon but now cannot stand to smell or eat it, others can observe her behavior, evidence of something gone temporarily awry in the way a woman reacts to food. This is a problem of self-understanding. What made me become a person who does not like bacon? It is a reasonable thing to wonder. Why should a sexual experience a few weeks before make a woman gag a few weeks later at the odor of frying bacon, which she normally loves, or make her seek out olives, which she normally avoids? The logical connections do not present themselves. An answer—"it's hormones"—has to be taken on faith since observation hardly suggests hormones as explanation for that weirdness. Nor is it obvious why the impending arrival of another person in the household (doesn't *he* like bacon?) causes the change.

Maternal impressions and folklore about cravings once provided reasonable answers to those reasonable questions. Rapunzel's mother wants rapunzel salad, that pungent herb, because her baby girl in utero wants it. Pregnant women crave coffee or strawberries or figs because the baby needs them. In premodern writings, after all, that treatment of cravings gave a reasonable explanation of why the new tastes varied so much from a woman's regular ones: they were strange because it actually could be the fetus, not the woman, who was savoring or despising those things. Most medically informed advice in our time has excluded that explanation.

While a woman's attitude to food during pregnancy is among the more visible shifts in her identity, doctors and guide-writers by mid-twentieth century routinely waved aside the mysteries of pregnant digestion. Robert Walsh tells pregnant readers that "nausea is not necessary," but rather is manageable by mere distraction: "tests have proved that if a person can take her mind off her condition, the sense of nausea will diminish or disappear entirely. So try to read a good, gripping novel. Watch television. . . . Or figure out other ways to get your mind off your condition for a time." Some guidebooks more or less told women that morning sickness was their own fault. Some guide-writers rendered it practically a moral obligation not to have morning sickness. Our current dietary advice might be sounder than its predecessors, but current advice evades rather than resolves the puzzle of why the pregnant body wants what it wants. Food may be the thing that makes a pregnant woman most aware of possessing appetites not her own.[5]

Though old explanations for cravings and nausea were quashed by respectable medicine, these notions kept popping up again in different guises. Nicholson Eastman admits it is "common knowledge that the early weeks of pregnancy are frequently associated with some degree of nausea." Eastman knows pregnant women could feel queasy for one reason that nonpregnant people do as well, a psychological reason. Eastman allows that "an upset mind may produce an upset stomach," and who, Eastman wonders, has more cause to have an upset mind than a woman expecting a baby? "Now, in all life's encounters there are probably few experiences which are at first more upsetting, mentally and emotionally, than the realization by a young woman that she is pregnant." Showing empathy with the potential worries of expectant women, Eastman reminds readers that "the implications of pregnancy extend far back into the past" and "its future ramifications are endless."

In this case Eastman credits rational calculation, rather than a powerful imagination, for making a woman feel sick.[6]

Cyril Pink locates the source of nausea even deeper in the tangled movements of identity and relationship occasioned by pregnancy. Nausea, he theorizes, might be caused by particular people or the way those people make the pregnant woman feel. In a guess that encapsulates a good many of the identity puzzles of pregnancy, Pink observes, "rarely we meet with a patient who can gladly face the world with her pregnancy but suffers from sickness as soon as she gets into the company of one individual." Pink concedes that a woman's pregnancy changes interactions with others. The upset caused by changes in those interactions and in the person she is presumed to be literally make her sick. Provocatively Pink continues: "In most of these cases a mother-in-law, who maintains a hostile attitude toward her, veiled or undisguised, is the cause of the trouble." Pink's anonymous patient's unfortunate mother-in-law may stand in for the whole range of people whose expectations and judgments change the person a pregnant woman may feel herself to be, and the relationships she has with others. What Pink calls a "wrong attitude towards reproduction" could be a trap for women who find themselves as wives expected to embrace intimacy they may have avoided, even feared, before.[7]

To be sure, this pregnant woman's in-laws have grounds for their interest in this fruit of the womb. The childbearing woman is carrying forth the lineage, the DNA, of her parents, in-laws, grandparents, and a great host of others. This fact too bears on a woman's identity. While there are exceptions, many of us do not ordinarily go about day by day thinking about ourselves in relation to the genes we carry. More often we imagine connections to forebears in terms of family, name, place, or quirk, and only secondarily in terms of genes. Even then, genes oftener seem to be what we are stuck with, what makes us ourselves, rather than the inherited parcel we have to tote around until we disburse it. While pregnant, a woman is urged to see herself as an agent tasked with handing on that stuff. This passive transmission of genetic material could be used to reassure worried pregnant women. Nicholson Eastman can reassure mothers that baby's mental characteristics "were determined in good measure when his grandparents married"—an expression that simultaneously attacks maternal impressions and incidentally minimizes good prenatal behavior. But a pregnant woman may wish she had more authority over this genetic material. A childbearing woman has to pass on to the child not what she wants or has earned but what she got. She cannot pass along only the best of herself, or construct a fetus out of what she wishes she had. Short of new techniques to trim the genes of our offspring, a pregnant woman here is conduit rather than cultivator.[8]

Transmitting DNA repositions the woman in terms of the coming child who will have her to thank or blame for genetic stuff, but also those who gave her that stuff in the first place. It is a convention of pregnancy advice manuals that expectant mothers get reflective about their own childhood and the parenting they received, that they worry about whether they will be good mothers in part with reference to their own. What the expectant mother does in her body allows her ancestors to have relationship with someone else who does not yet exist. Thus pregnancy requires taking stock of what Leon Kass calls linkage and lineage, the way the body itself beckons us to look back to those we came from, and ahead to those who will follow, in an immediate, self-conscious way.[9]

Linking together those who came before with those who will come after her is a self-abnegating position. Reproducing is, in Kass's words, "voting with your feet for your own demise." Mortality is bound up with childbearing, in some ways abstractly, in other ways immediately, one's ancestors' mortality, one's own, even that of one's offspring. The mother stands in relation to the child as giver of life, bestower of the genetic materials that form a unique life, yes, but also as one customarily credited with giving the child a mortal body, a finite span. Life as a mortal creature means being one who will die, rather than being a disembodied eternal soul. Bearing children into life means burdening them with bodies that disintegrate and decay. The baby's clock starts ticking down within her body, before she even knows the beating has started. When a child comes to life in the body of the mother, that is the beginning of the end—an idea that has long resonance in Western thought about childbearing. In her mid-twentieth-century manual of fetal development, Margaret Shea Gilbert observes, "Death throws its shadow over man before he is born, for the stream of life flows most swiftly through the embryo as a young fetus, and then inexorably slows down, even within the uterus."[10]

Perhaps this sounds morbid. Certainly the expectant woman should not have to shoulder blame for the whole life of the not-yet-born child, the eventual aging and decay of the one she carries new into the world. (Prenatal care scaremongering can foster this kind of self-blame when it warns, like Josephine Baker, "Upon the health of the mother during the pregnant period may depend the entire health and well being of her child throughout its life.") Even in the happiest of birth scenarios, the mother beholding her child quails at a world rife with accidents and dangers that threaten that fragile body. And in the more bitter birth scenarios, death within the frame of birth has immediacy instead of a long glance to inevitable decline. Common estimates suggest that between 10 and 25 percent of pregnancies end in miscarriage. Actual numbers cannot be known since some of these, "chemical pregnancies," end before anyone is aware of them. The actual numbers could be much higher. In times past when it was virtually impossible to know whether an egg was fertilized or not, it was hard to distinguish a late period from an early miscarriage. Now with pregnancy revealed early and with knowledge of fetal development familiar to the man on the street, women may choose to recognize and mourn what is lost, or not. Miscarriage, as Leslie Reagan traces, was not always mourned as a tragedy, but could come as a relief, as God's or nature's way of averting problems with babies who could not have survived.[11]

For the pregnant woman, the capacity to bear a person into the world alive is paired with the capacity to carry death. She might carry death not just in the general human sense that we are all mortal, but in her living out of pregnancies that do not work. How a woman experiences a miscarriage depends partially on her view and experience of the pregnancy. A woman visibly and perceptibly pregnant for months may discover at some point that the fetus is no longer alive. An ultrasound might find no fetal heartbeat. Until the fetus is removed by natural or medical process, for some time the woman's body harbors the lifeless body of the baby. Her temporary condition is to live while holding someone else's death. Pregnancy presupposes willingness to do this, whether or not the event happens in any particular pregnancy. Carrying, accepting, mourning, and separating from the death of a fetus impresses the identity of the bearing woman.[12]

### Relationship

Disorienting to the self, childbearing can also shift relationships with others, from the relationship the woman has within the space of her own body to those she maintains with all others. As a condition of constant contact between the woman and another, pregnancy is a remarkable relationship. If we admit this coexistence is the case—that we did not come to be by springing up like fungi but came in the context of other embodied relationships—pregnancy helps us observe it in practice.

Even superficial interactions with strangers can change during pregnancy. Strangers may offer the pregnant woman a seat on a bus, let her go ahead in line to the bathroom, open a door on her behalf. Though this seems negligible, it reflects a significant change in others' responses to her based on assumptions about her condition. Past the fifth month or so, onlookers know right away what a woman's condition is. Otherwise they scrutinize. Is that woman just wearing a big shirt? While it can feel rude or intrusive, this gaze, as Florentien Verhage insists, is complex in its intention and reception. The pregnant woman simultaneously can be conspicuous and unseen. The woman may feel very visible but also as though onlookers try to look past or around her bulk in order to see the fetus: "the pregnant woman can hardly hide her body from the world, she is visually overdetermined as 'with child.'"[13]

Even the possibility that a woman might be pregnant can bring new reactions from beholders. Admittedly it can be an awkward transaction, as Elizabeth Yuko reports in a *New York Times* reflection, "When You Look Pregnant, but You're Not." Yuko finds mortification the norm when someone decides to notice in public a woman's big belly or loose dress, worse when the judgment is mistaken ("Congratulations! When are you due?"). Yuko's article drew over 1200 comments, many recommending that observers keep mouths shut rather than mistakenly offering a seat or a compliment. Politeness might make reticence the right choice. On the other hand, there are reasons to justify pausing to puzzle over the perhaps pregnant figure. That awkward moment, wondering whether that person is or is not, offers an opportunity to rethink what we see, to see rightly. That split second of paying attention is important. It is especially important if followed up by action that demonstrates regard for the bearing of new life. Americans do not excel in showing deference to anyone. Women on subways do not usually announce pregnancy in order to get free seats. But small stirrings of politesse are important, the germ of something that can be coaxed into actual appreciation for what that pregnant woman is doing. What the big-bellied body might suggest to us is not just the fact of the fetus, but the work-in-process of the woman, the significance of her carriage. The fact that women do this should be arresting to all who watch it, since all come to be because, structurally, such a relationship exists. One respondent to Yuko's article, identifying herself as "NYC Mom," gave voice to such a sentiment:

> In this city of anonymous faces rushing by every day, I found it a joy that people would take an extra moment to smile and nod at me when I was pregnant. I felt a strong spiritual connection to the universe and had the sense that others wanted to share that with me, just for a moment. It was icing on the cake. I understand that pregnancy is a private experience and not everyone wants to share it. But, for me, NYC became a more friendly place when I was pregnant and I loved it.

Certainly, any doubt about pregnant status might recommend reticence on the part of passersby. Still, cultivating recognition matters in a culture where childbearing gets treated lightly.[14]

As historian Ulinka Rublack demonstrates, pregnant women in early modern Germany had a public role and a certain kind of power. They were permitted to seek better conditions for themselves—

requesting city intervention to be sure they got sufficient food and avoided abuse—and also for others, allowed make extraordinary petitions for clemency for criminals sentenced to death. This is not to suggest that women were better understood or esteemed in sixteenth-century Europe. Instead, we admit that others in a different time and place recognized something we sometimes overlook. Women were granted special privileges when pregnant because they were doing something significant, of import not only to their private households but to the city at large. Perhaps we retain this assumption residually: reporter Cokie Roberts, describing her confrontation with police violence at the 1968 Democratic convention in Chicago, recalls, "I was very pregnant, so I was able to sort of stand the cops down a little bit."[15]

Pregnancy can affect relationships with other women, from the most generalized sisterhood to friends and relatives. Sometimes it will tip relationships with friends, the pregnancy of one causing grief to another in the midst of infertility, or drawing a woman nearer to one also expecting or caring for a new baby. Not only in casual relationships but in closer ones, self-awareness about carrying a child can induce adjustments. Those may see the most change.

"There will be permanent changes in your relations with your husband after your return from the hospital with the baby. The baby should unify—not divide—his parents," a Catholic guide advises. In many ways situation-specific enough to confound all attempts to generalize, the relationship between the bearer of a child and the begetter of it, woman and man, may transform as they approach roles as mother and father. Their affinity may grow deeper as they engage in the project of raising children. Or instead, one or the other might recoil at childrearing, perhaps not wishing for eros to be interrupted by a kid, or for a host of other reasonable hesitations. The very prospect of birth can alter the relationship. Michael Banner argues, "the child has now taken a signif-icance in cementing relationships that were previously cemented by sexual intercourse—It's a child of *our* own which makes *us* us, whereas once it was the sexual union of flesh which served that purpose."[16]

In a union with ambitions to permanence, a couple may delight to think their bodily love may yield a child. In other situations, the poten-tial of sex to end up as reproduction can be felt as a conflict. The pur-poses and consequences of sex, what Roman Catholic moral theology usefully names the "goods of marriage," can be linked together in some ways that are better than others. While this terminology of "goods" has particular meaning and obligation for Catholics, it is useful for others because it assists consideration of pregnancy's effects on marital rela-tionships. For Catholics, the "unitive good" of marriage denotes the erotic love that brings a couple closer together, eros in enjoyment and physical union. The "procreative good" is the name for the capacity of sex to produce babies. The schema has the benefit of connecting two important features of embodied love. A glance at the erotic advice pre-sented in mass-market magazines clustered around drugstore counters suggests that plenty of us (at least plenty of the young, attractive people on magazine covers) prefer to make no conceptual link between sex acts and progeny in coital behavior. Until we want to.

Many of us at some point do want to describe who we are, who our children are, with something like those terms. Perhaps especially in answering a child's question about where babies come from, some people still like the explanation that a child's existence comes from parents' love for each other and from desire for a child-to-be—both of those things, wound together, a coherent pair of desires constitutive of new life. Well into the early modern period, common belief held that both man and woman had to reach orgasm for a sexual encounter to be fertile. Troubling though that idea is, factually wrong, theoretically awful, and wide open to abuse, it can be read as an attempt by pre-moderns to explain how offspring came from union. Literature, art, history, and social science all contribute testimonies of the difficulty of keeping together the unitive and procreative purposes of sex. To be sure, women can become pregnant absent love or consent. Moral teaching, Roman Catholic or not, may declare that unitive and procreative aspects of sex should be held together. Pregnancy goes theology one better. Pregnancy supplies the defect of the bare words. These declarations *say* that the two aspects should be together, but the body of the pregnant woman actually *shows* it. The body of the pregnant woman unites the unitive and procreative, as the same organs that draw desire produce and bring forth a child.

## Maternal-Fetal Relationship

Beyond the spousal relationship, the connection between woman and fetus looks closer than pretty much any other human connection. But this proximity has been regularly dismissed. Old prescriptive literature, especially medical manuals, insisted mother and fetus were totally separate. That assumption of distance sprang partly from excusable anatomical misunderstanding and partly from revulsion at what must lie on the other side of a woman's belly button, and what indignities must be endured before human beings emerge "between feces and urine," in the attribution of St. Augustine. The womb sits between "the most filthy and vile excrements which exist in the body," is an "inconstant" organ, humans "enter[ing] the world from out of a sewer," in some early modern estimations.[17]

Though writers of midwifery manuals knew that birth was a mess, a ruckus and a flood, many illustrations of the fetus-in-utero show a striking consistency in depicting a quiet, remote fetal apartment, secluded from the surrounding mother. In some of these medieval and early modern images, fetuses jump, squat, dance in an empty space where no other objects block their movement. The fetal figures in these illustrations usually are large, well-formed, nearly whole children, chubby active boys with luxuriant heads of hair. In depictions of twins, the two appear to be enjoying each other's company, sometimes holding hands, sometimes even making eye contact with the viewer, rather than looking to the mother for anything. Most of the time, fetal space has literally nothing to do with the actual body of a woman, as though the uterus were a free-floating bubble.[18]

Some more recent illustrations situate a fetus in a uterus that *is* perceptibly a place in the body of a woman. Some still draw the woman's uterus as though viewed through the skin, a window onto the womb, with the rest of the woman cut off or blurred out. Sketches of a fetus-in-a-female-trunk still imply that the child is sealed off from the woman's guts, thoughts, emotions. In word and image interpreters emphasize that mother and child have no direct contact, quite obsessive in denying direct contact of blood or nerves. "There is no direct connection between mother and baby either by nerve, tissue or blood," Castallo and Walz inveigh, hitting a note common to this literature. Explaining how nutrients pass through the umbilical cord, which they liken to a tree trunk (presumably rooted in maternal soil through the placenta) they stress, "[t]here is no other connection."[19]

In past or present, drawings that portray a fetus in solitude mislead, since a healthy fetus is never disconnected from its mother before birth readiness except in case of abnormality, abortion, or danger. One implication of pictures that represent a faraway fetus is to deny a relationship between the two. As Cynthia D. Coe observes, "[t]he child's relation to the mother is unseverable but subject to a double concealment— buried, and the fact of the burial itself covered over."[20]

But woman and fetus are very close, together under the skin. That closeness is one basis for describing maternal-fetal interaction as a relationship. Recognizing this, that we each are not cast generally into the human lot but come first tied—literally—to a particular woman, James Mumford argues, "Maternal testimony bears witness to human beings having been thrown into (1) a relationship which is *particular* and (2) a relationship which is *asymmetrical*, that is, in which one 'party' comes to be wholly dependent upon the other." The "relationship between mother and child is itself unique," Lisa Guenther argues, for "I will never dwell in the body of any other person but my mother; I will never again share this sort of intimacy with someone, this dense intertwining of 'accident, innocence and indebtedness.'" The mother is giving, and is aware of giving, whether or not the child's reactions correspond in ways akin to other relationships. Irina Aristarkhova insists that gifts go both ways: "Hospitality requires both giving and receiving, and it is important to note that there is more to this relation than the mother's receipt of the rejected waste from the guest of the matrix." The exchange is reciprocal though not equal. On the physical level the woman sustains and maintains the fetus, but both exchange cells, respond to touch, share the placenta, share this experience.[21]

Of course, imagining a relationship does not make it so, and women might not be interested in understanding their carriage of fetus-in-utero as some kind of relationship. Still, since long assumptions of physical distance and mental disconnection have been pitted against this understanding of a maternal-fetal relationship, some good reasons exist to take it seriously. In her chapter handling "Pregnancy as a Relationship," Barbara Katz Rothman rejects the conventional imagery sharpening the divide between mother and fetus. The fact that we all "unfold" from one another is among the most stunning features of human life.[22]

Further, the fact of this relationship is not undone by its partially imagined character. Even before it became common for parents-to-be to discover the sex of an awaited child, but all the more since, many expectant parents have enjoyed speculating about the personality of coming David or Emily, referring to the fetus by the name they select, ascribing characteristics to the fetus based on their ambitions or the mother's perceptions of kicks and somersaults. A tendency fostered by family planning and fetal imaging, the socially favored approach for wanted pregnancies now casts the nine months as a kind of long-term snuggle with a beloved pet. The woman may perceive responses to her own relational efforts. It now is common knowledge that the fetus both receives and responds to stimuli while in utero. From observing movement and heart rate, researchers have documented fetal responses to maternal actions.

Reluctance to apply the name relationship to those interactions may hang more with our incomprehension of fetal behavior than with lack of real fetal response. Studies from the last decade show that fetus and mother actually do engage in mysterious contact, explicable in full neither by experience nor biology though perceptible by both. Research demonstrates that infants recognize the mother's voice, can distinguish between the language used by the mother before birth from a foreign language, and respond to touch most of all. To be sure, a relationship with a fetus is not exactly the same as other relationships. But its peculiarities do not negate its status as a relationship. Further, while much imagery of mother and fetus emphasizes their distance, folklore and miracle stories tell of children speaking from the womb, of embryonic saints passing judgment, even of a seven-month fetus in Revolutionary France singing the Ça Ira.[23]

How does a woman build a relationship with someone whom she cannot see but is closer to her than her own skin? Through physical accommodation, thinking about the child, preparation on the child's behalf, the woman develops something recognizable as a relationship. Women experiment with behaviors, some similar to those appropriate in other relationships, others distinct. They may talk or sing to the fetus, then wait or listen for responses. A woman might try to touch the fetus in a particular way, rubbing her own abdomen or holding her hands in a position resembling an embrace. This specially intended touch is familiar in some circles as a way for mothers—and others—to interact with the baby under the woman's skin. People figure this out all by themselves, of course, but systems also exist to render the gesture more purposeful.

Some French and British natural childbirth proponents recommend "haptonomy" to teach a kind of emotionally directed laying on of hands. Calling it "bonding, the French way," a UK antenatal services group describes it as a "way to develop a loving relationship with your baby through pregnancy." With evidence from ultrasound images showing that the fetus will cuddle up to hands placed over the abdomen, advocates of this technique insist that touch can foster relationships with baby-to-be. Not from holistic sensibilities but from training in Catholic theology, William D. Virtue promotes haptonomy for expectant women, counseling them to fetal communication by gentle pressure exerted by both hands on either side of the navel. This sort of counsel makes sense. But it also carries a whiff of the ridiculous, an effort to choreograph a movement a woman often would do anyway untutored. Further, this choreographed touch undervalues the touch pregnant women already give fetuses constantly, simply in the fact of gestation.[24]

Touch is the basis of a woman's relationship with the fetus. Stressing the importance of sensory connection in building relationship, Florentien Verhage describes pregnancy as a "nonfrontal embrace between two separate but connected entities." A relationship between woman and baby does not commence at delivery, but instead "*before* birth the pregnant woman already interacts with the growing fetus, most prominently through touch." Indeed, Verhage gives definition, "to be pregnant means continually to be touching and being touched." A woman's caress of her own abdomen does not touch the baby directly but respects the collaborative character of a human's coming-to-be. The rubbing of one's own abdomen at once intends the caress for the fetus and for her own stretched belly carrying the fetus. The presence of the child in the mother's physical space underscores the fact of our coexistence, the necessity of relationships as means of moving in human life.[25]

Premodern models of fetal behavior sometimes suggested that a fetus calls all the shots—building up a body, taking what she needs from the bloodstream, dumping his wastes into maternal removal systems—while the mother remains apart, mind elsewhere, only mechanically attendant. Finding no apparent conduit from the mother's brain to the fetal one, pregnancy advice writers conclude you can't get there from here. A very few advice writers in the late nineteenth century still affirm maternal impressions; among them Prudence Saur was confident that women could impart "tendencies" to the baby. In a startling fusion of newer discoveries and antique embryology, Saur summarizes reproduction this way: the embryo's "structural basis" comes from the father but "is formed and developed in all its parts, even to the minutest details" by "action of the vital, mental and spiritual forces of the mother." Saur thinks it certainly is "within the mother's power, by the voluntary and intelligent direction of her own forces . . . to shape the mental, moral and spiritual features of her child to an extent to which no limit may be assigned," so the "psychological influence of such aspirations" are unquestionable.[26]

Even as they advised against maternal anxiety, some guidebook writers anticipated what scientists discovered recently and are still discovering. Pathways made by chemical signals from maternal actions, like fear or stress, get communicated to the fetus through the bloodstream. This admission is like the missing piece of a road map. Mom's worries or weird ideas are her own problem, insist twentieth-century guidebooks, you can't get there from here. Reminding readers that "no nerves whatsoever run from the mother's body to that of the unborn babe" and dismissing the umbilical cord as having "no more function than a hose-pipe," Bernarr Macfadden scoffs at the woman who "reads beautiful books, sings lovely songs, and gazes at wonderful pictures." In fact, to "impress" the child, thoughts or emotions need not travel from the mother's brain to the baby's brain, but take the detour through the mother's blood to the child's circulation. Even though a fetus may not feel fear because her mother felt fear, the fetal body feels chemical reactions to the mother's fear, and reacts. These signals contribute to the pattern of actions and responses comprising the relationship between woman and fetus.[27]

The relationship between childbearing woman and fetus is not like most other human relationships but is fundamental to making possible all the rest of them. That causal sequence, mother nurturing fetus to enable baby's future capacities in service of others, is illustrated in an astonishing speech that Carolyn Van Blarcom puts in the mouth of a newborn. Encouraging the woman to breastfeed, her just-born child tells his mother his good intentions: "now I want to go on and develop the best possible mind and body. I shall be able to do this if you will help me, for what you can give me now is of more importance than what all the rest of the people in the world can give." The child is asking for breast milk. Strikingly, Van Blarcom's articulate baby identifies this special food as a woman's unique contribution to his flourishing. This comes with irony since breast milk, technically, can be provided by another woman, while the gestational care from which the child has just emerged had as yet no substitution. (We may recognize surrogacy as a norm but Van Blarcom's audience would not have done so.) Begging the mother's investment for a while longer in order to pay it back in multiples later, the child requests, "Just tide me over this most difficult period of my life and I'll be a credit to us both, not only as a baby but as a growing child . . . helping to do my share of the world's work." It is a curious speech in a number of ways. It highlights the particular claim and requirement a particular child has of a particular woman, amplified by the larger contribution the woman makes by serving a child who goes on to serve the world. But the child already plans to pay it forward. The imaginary newborn expresses desire to honor the woman's relationship with him by being "a credit to us both."[28]

Relationships and self-understanding can be difficult to detangle in pregnancy. Not only does the fetus respond to the mother's relational gestures while in utero, but registers permanently its presence in the mother's body. That is, carrying a fetus changes who the woman *is*. This change is not mere imagination. It happens on the cellular level. Childbearing induces microchimerism, a condition wherein an organ-

ism is composed of cells from more than one individual. During gestation mother and fetus each transfer cells to the body of the other; the
fetus not only is composed of the mixed DNA inheritance from both
parents, not only is nurtured in the tissues of the mother, but keeps
some of her cells in its body. The mother can retain stray fetal DNA in
her bloodstream and fetal cells in some somatic tissues for decades after
the child is born. In 2015 researchers assessed this microchimerism as a
"tug-of-war," between the two, characterized by both cooperation and
conflict. A team of researchers describes the transfer this way:

> During pregnancy, there is a bi-directional flow of fetal and maternal
> cells. The transfer of these cells is asymmetrical, with more fetal cells
> being transferred to the mother than vice versa. Fetal cells increase in
> frequency in the maternal body with increasing gestational age and
> have been identified in maternal blood and tissues for decades fol-
> lowing birth. After parturition, the maternal immune system actively
> clears some but not all fetal cells from the maternal blood through in-
> ducing apoptosis. Maternal microchimerism (the transfer of maternal
> cells to the fetus) is commonly found in fetal tissues as well, and also
> persist for decades after birth. Microchimerism is not thought to be
> limited to just the bi-directional exchange of mother and fetal cells:
> cells from older siblings and even maternal grandmother cells might
> also be transferred to the fetus.[29]

What microchimerism implies is startling, though not entirely
surprising, science in a way confirming what experience suggests. It
takes Rothman's phrase describing pregnancy as relationship one step
further: we do not only unfold from each other, we remain in and of
each other persistently. Women who have been pregnant are no longer

just themselves. This revelation of our cellular sharing, microscopic evidence of the already evident overlap of our lives, ought to refresh imagination about that female figure protruding a bump. Until such time as gestation outside the womb is normalized, the existence of each of us in the world depends on this relationship of care. We are, all of us, marked by the experience of pregnancy, whether or not we have ourselves been pregnant. A little awe is in order.

CONCLUSION

# *Pregnancy beyond Metaphor*

Once the baby is born, the family, the community, and society at large come to recognize and absorb the new child.... But before all this, it is time to pause for a moment, as did Eve, and reflect on what has happened: "For I, with God, have created a human."

—Tikva Frymer-Kensky, *Motherprayer* (1996)

It is said that in the civilization of ancient Greece things were managed better; thus it was customary for pedestrians to show great respect to an expectant mother and a stranger would often hand her a flower, or some trifle of beauty.

—Cyril V. Pink, *The Foundations of Motherhood* (1947)

I t might seem strange that a hill town in the Italian countryside would find it necessary to pay people to live there. Who wouldn't want to live in an Italian hill town, with that food, that light, that view, that dolce vita? Attractive as they still are to visit, these dreamy villages have less draw as places to make a life. In 2003 Laviano, a town in the southern Italian region of Campania, feeling the pain of population reduction, offered 10,000 euros for resident women who carried a pregnancy to term. The bounty was not for the childbearing itself, exactly, but for the baby and for the pledge to stay in town after the birth. The goal of the payment was to boost the shrinking demographics (around 1500) of the very small and scenically located town. Laviano's population-building disbursements would come to parents when the baby was born and at subsequent birthdays until the child's start of school. The town's policy seems not to have yielded much, since Laviano's population now is smaller than in 2003. Still, this very local solution expresses something poignant, neighbors frankly admitting to each other that the flourishing of all depends on this very specific task that some women do for reasons beyond cash and civic pride.[1]

Even when parents can really use the money, baby bonuses can be awkward. State payments to boost population may feel off-putting even if not entirely offensive, because payments suggest somehow that breeding might be reducible to money, open to easy manipulation and regulation by governments—likelier a premise for dystopian literature than for popular policy. A 2018 editorial in an official newspaper in China catches this awkwardness when, after years devoted to slowing population growth by its one-child policy, the country began struggling to persuade families to have more children: "To put it bluntly, the birth of a baby is not only a matter of the family itself, but also a state affair." That is not to say some natalist policies are not popular. Some countries give payments and tax breaks, maternity and paternity leaves, or subsidies for childcare. In Finland, mothers-to-be can elect either cash or a cardboard box of supplies. Finland's baby box is so popular that families in other countries have adopted it as a trendy and safe receptacle for newborns. To be sure, these gestures are not just about babies or making them, but aim to demonstrate that the government, or people speaking through their government, wish to be friendly to families.[2]

In Italy the problem is not isolated to Laviano or small towns like it. Pronatalist efforts can disturb with the crude implication that children are borne for the state, women prized for their capacity to multiply soldiers or workers, Junior called into being so his earnings can provide upkeep for his grandparents' pension. Further, natalist policies can disturb when set against growth elsewhere on the globe or the immigration of people with higher birth rates. The challenges of providing for all the earth's people make questionable paid efforts to generate more Europeans. People move out of charming but dying little towns to have babies elsewhere because economic and cultural shifts make one place more promising than another to raise children into maturity. When a family is expanding, parents may welcome financial or practical assistance. State and corporate provisions in the United States sometimes look substandard when compared to generous offerings given in other countries. Even so, problems attend both the idea and execution of these policies as ways of respecting the work of pregnancy. Most women do not decide to have babies because somebody gives them a tax break or cash payment.[3]

What governments can do with money by way of regarding pregnancy may be more limited, anyway, than what the market might provide. Looking for a way to honor a pregnant woman? Why not buy her something? Somebody selling something would be glad to oblige.

In hopes of profit, marketers have directed all kinds of merchandise at expectant women. But to their own loss, sellers seem as narrow in vision about what pregnancy entails as is the culture at large. Maternity merchandise is overwhelmed by baby junk. The market is glad to oblige with more stuff, but does not offer the right stuff.

To do better, in terms of stuff or manners or gestures, we must start by thinking better. The clearing away of mistaken embryology allowed doctors and the rest of us to realize that the bearing of new life calls forth estimable work on the part of the woman involved. Previous chapters of this book considered what kind of activity this is, and how reflection about it might help us appreciate our character as creatures dependent on each other in this way. As women practice this fetal nurture for nine months, they may reshape aspects of themselves, not only deepening prudence, courage, charity, hospitality, but demonstrating them to those with eyes to see. Doing all this has potential to adjust the identity of one doing it and enrich relationships with others.

Baby bonuses, family leave policies, and stuff can be desirable but are not chiefly what is desired by way of marking the import of child-bearing. Even the soft benefits sometimes socially available to pregnant women, like special seating on buses and trains or "stork" parking spaces nearest to grocery stores, run the risk of causing offense rather than being perceived as positive. What else is there to do?

### Can OBs Oversee This Part of Pregnancy?

Perhaps doctors, the people to whom Americans predominantly entrust things birth related, can offer women not only safety and health but also gestures of respect. Some surely do. Some might do better.

As a standard practice, OB offices could send flower arrangements to all their newly delivered patients, first thing. But doing much more than that might not be reasonable to expect. Doctors are not really in that line of work. Paradoxically, the very success of the prenatal care approach may make it harder to honor women's prenatal efforts. Leaving matters to the doctor makes the doctor responsible for the interpretation of pregnancy, removes motivation for women to think about it outside doctors' purview. Because women may not have any other means to describe the work they are doing in pregnancy besides following doctors' orders, they may feel they are working to no point. Of course, few obstetricians would intend to convey this to patients, but the implication suggests itself: we give you these little jobs to make you feel like you are helping out, but the real work is on us.

Language showing the shift from pregnancy interpreted by culture to pregnancy interpreted by science may be accurate, but the language of medicine is itself a historical artifact. As we have seen, discussion of pregnancy ideas from earlier periods observes nuance and insight in ways that current language excludes, not because nuance is gone but because our vocabulary has changed. Current-day maternity explanations are no more outside of history than old-fashioned ones, though they sometimes get presented as such. For example, in an essay summarizing "Reproduction since 1750" in an academic history of sex and the body, a scholar first discusses old ideas reflecting ideologies of their time and place, eighteenth-century misogyny and medicine. But when she pivots to summarize understandings from 1750 to the present, historical consciousness falls away, and biology simply *is*:

> The way the human body in general and the female body in particular were understood changed markedly during the period under consid-

eration. Basic anatomy became better understood, particularly as microscopy improved. Spermatozoa and then the mammalian egg were observed, then chromosomes (the string-like material within a cell's nucleus) were also seen. In the early twentieth century knowledge of genetics and the role of genes in heredity were developed, until in 1953 the structure of DNA was discovered. . . . We know now that the human female reproductive cycle lasts around 21 to 35 days. Doctors take the beginning of menstruation as the start date for the cycle. . . . Ovulation takes place roughly mid-cycle when there is a thick vascular lining to the womb.[4]

Even making allowance for the background-sketching function of such prose, its explanations are jarring. The writing relies heavily on passive voice. In it, changes mostly just happen—things were seen, bodies were understood—rather than being thought or wrought by some persons and received or resisted by others. Steps in the march of scientific progress claim no complexity. These reproductive processes simply *are*. Complexities get overridden by statements of fact: *We know now*. History itself recedes. Still, it is worth remembering that medical procedures themselves function as rituals, replacing rather than just displacing folk customs. Anthropologists of American birth point out that the protocols of hospital birth are not all simply medically necessary but act as "rites of passage." Sizing a woman's belly with a tape measure in routine prenatal visits, or fastening a fetal heart monitor to a woman's abdomen during labor, have power as rituals just as did the act of tying to the laboring woman's thigh a scroll reading, "Lazarus, Come out!"[5]

Learning to recognize some hospital labor-and-delivery procedures as rituals allows a fresh view of the central problem of the prenatal experience. If many of the procedures and behaviors recommended for pregnancy are not necessary or not necessarily effective, why should women's nine months be shaped by them? Things like birth classes might be mere artifacts of a transitional time, between periods when people thought pregnancy was passive and when they began relying heavily on doctors to make babies come out safely at the end.

In the late 1960s, a scholar of birth practices in Australia puzzled over why women still put effort into prenatal preparations even though by then obstetrics had rendered those maternal efforts unnecessary through procedures making delivery safer and less painful. Surveying natural childbirth exercises that already looked outdated to her in the 1960s, Adele Blankfield theorizes, "Faced by the perils of parturition, different preparations for childbirth were originally undertaken to procure a healthy mother and baby." Blankfield sees, as we see, that obstetric medicine by the early twentieth century understood some problems but had not yet discovered how to make labor reliably safe and painless. Doctors in this period knew more about reproduction than, say, Aristotle, but not enough to optimize everyone's results. Some practitioners sought to alleviate this tension by giving women tasks to contribute. Preparative exercises for the mother filled the gap left between medicine's understanding of birth problems and its inability to solve them: "As medical science appeared not to be forthcoming with dramatic solutions to these problems, people empirically claimed various dietetic and physical means to be of value."[6]

At this writing, birth techniques and medicine are far beyond the level achieved in the 1960s, but Blankfield's insight can yet inform the paradoxes of pregnancy and birth. Medical advances rendered unnecessary the behaviors that medicine assigned to pregnant women. Women could continue doing these things if they felt like it, but all those funny exercises lost their point once delivery technology changed: "to our society with its obstetrical advances, it is an anachronism." Birth could be left to doctors:

> Since the solution to the mortality problems have been found, many older ideas were discarded and physiotherapy became a fringe subject with little medical guidance. Thus the idea of training for an easy, painless, unassisted birth without complication, still persists. This philosophy has become invalid as preparation is proved not to have an effect on the form of labour or the occurrence of complications.[7]

Since Blankfield's day, doctors now provide even more rules along with more urgent justifications. Instead of elevating the appraisal of women's prenatal work, those advisories induce a sort of paralysis. But this need not be the last word. Epigenetics attests to the significance of women's prenatal behaviors on the lifelong health of offspring. What women do during pregnancy matters. Doctors do many important things for expectant parents and babies. But doctors and hospitals may not be well suited to explain the human import of that experience. No more than state or market, the obstetric profession might not be ideally suited to the task of observing pregnancy as morally significant work. The task falls to culture.

### What We Already Have: Showers, Robes, and Casseroles

A human phenomenon as self-evidently important as death, childbearing deserves to be honored with cultural gestures. We have gestures to mark other aspects of embodied life, like sex, eating, aging, fitness, sickness. We have many ways to honor or suffer these other experiences but lack them for pregnancy. Because pregnancy can reshape relationships among the mother and others, it would be desirable that people surrounding an expectant woman have some appropriate way to respond, to recognize this as more than a private event. It may be tempting to invent something new. But new rituals are hard to make stick. They often look ridiculous: you want me to do *what* for my pregnant neighbor? We might first take stock of what we already have, now or in practices that could be recovered from the past.

Something old, something new, and something borrowed: Americans already have parties focused on expectant parents, gifts for mothers-to-be. We might find something useful among practices current in other cultures. We sometimes refresh old gestures through new technologies. Religion offers some rituals for pregnancy, some of which have been popularized through adaptation by others outside the faith. Some Hindus honor mothers-to-be in the seventh month, hoping for safety through birth. A Navajo rite has been adapted by some American women into a ceremony called a Blessing Way. Some Christian churches celebrate the feast of Annunciation with a nod to expectant mothers, marking the occasion when the promise of Jesus was made known to Mary with a blessing for pregnant women in the congregation.[8]

Some celebrations already common in the United States are better in theory than practice. The biggest fuss made over expectant mothers outside of the doctors' office usually comes with a baby shower. Baby showers illustrate the potential and the limits of extant gestures for recognizing pregnancy. Though they honor the pregnant woman, their chief focus is the not-yet-arrived one, with gifts and fanfare almost exclusively targeted to the coming infant. Showers get silly quickly. Baby showers can serve as a rite of passage in becoming a mother, the expectant woman welcomed into a fellowship of women as she receives their advice and wisdom. Generally though, gifts of advice now recede as presents pile on. Gifts can be spectacularly considerate, friends and family helping lower the cost of this monumental event. Having other people buy clothes, strollers, toys, and diapers reduces the amount that expectant parents have to spend themselves. Still, events oriented around giving gifts easily deteriorate into the merely commercial.[9]

Whose party is this? Focus usually stays firmly on the baby as guests and guest of honor admire gift after gift and imagine him or her wearing or playing with that thing. Those onesies or crib toys become a sort of prevenient grace, a pledge of long-term solicitude for a person before he or she even exists. That is a lovely purpose for a party. It does less well as the theme for a party celebrating the expectant woman. Like ultrasound images, showers tend to make the baby more visible by setting the woman aside. She sits as the body between the gifts and their recipient, unwrapping the presents for the person wrapped inside her. Reforming baby showers through comparisons to other sorts of parties might be desirable. If the baby is the guest of honor, the baby shower is like a housewarming. Gifts are given to help the coming person feel comfortable and equipped in the space they will be newly occupying. But if the pregnant woman is the guest of honor something different might be wanted, less like someone else's housewarming and more, perhaps, like a graduation party. At graduation parties, guests anticipate favorably the honoree's future, may applaud new ventures or challenges. But the focus of the celebration first is placed on the doings that brought the graduate up to that point. Graduation parties mark the end of an important piece of work. Something has been fulfilled. Whether it was painful or pleasant, whether or not all got done as hoped, that period draws to a close and ushers in an altogether new way of living. Maternity festivities could borrow that sensibility.

At baby showers the miniscule clothing unwrapped for baby contrasts dramatically with what the expectant woman often wears at such a party. It is perhaps not surprising that when Calvin University professor Debra Rienstra was pregnant and wanted something that would display the transformative "terrible aspect" of pregnancy, her thoughts turned to clothes. People still recognize the power of clothes to communicate significance. Clothes signal formal occasions, display membership, show honor. Wanting a special birthing robe, Tikva Frymer-Kensky finds the design obvious: lightweight, loose, short, with no fastenings, decorated with "appropriate sayings and designs," like "Holy to the Lord." Women could have two sets of these garments, one effectively like a hospital gown but designating birth rather than "ill health," and the other an elaborate keepsake to hand down to others, the way a christening gown or wedding dress might be, to be passed along to other women "preparing to enter the sacred realm of birth." Rienstra wishes that pregnant women would wear "elegant, drapey robes, like you would see on a Greek statue." It would be beautiful, she says, if "[h]ugely pregnant women could parade around, their gorgeous garments swirling behind them, and people would stop to stare and maybe bow their heads to acknowledge the Creator's power mirrored in the woman, and the woman would bow her head in return out of thanks that God has enabled her to mirror the poignance of bearing life." Not that Rienstra had such garments to put on at the time.[10]

When cloth was costly and many clothes handsewn, it made little sense to have a set of garments limited only to a few months' span of pregnancy. Off-the-rack maternity clothes are a relatively new invention. Through the nineteenth century in the United States women had skirts and undergarments that could accommodate increasing bulk. Dress reformers inveighed against the corset and its crushing of abdomens. Early twentieth-century garment pioneer Lena Himmelstein Bryant devised some of the earliest ready-made maternity clothes. Bryant, who became "Lane Bryant" when a bank misspelled the name on her account, used her skill as a seamstress to devise comfortable and attractive skirts and dresses for pregnant women. She opened her first store in 1904. In the late 1930s, Dallas sisters Edna, Elsie, and Louise Frankfurt made maternity clothes more elegant and businesslike with a unique design that went around the belly and kept hemlines even. The Frankfurts' label, Page Boy, sold stylish suits to starlets and other high-profile women expecting babies. Advice guides through the 1940s still assumed some women were sewing their own maternity outfits, though by midcentury they emphasized the availability of ready-made things as they assured women that pregnancy was no excuse for being badly dressed. While mass-marketed maternity wear went mainstream as the century progressed, fashions changed. Women now might visit maternity shops, but many women adapt regular wardrobes as long as they can rather than buying separate ones. Twenty-first century changes in tastes invited women to reveal the bump with close and clingy fabrics rather than draping it with voluminous ones.[11]

A glorious robe might be just what the pregnant woman wants to reflect the magnitude of her shape and work. But American women do not always love their maternity clothes. Maternity garments often enter a closet with a few strikes already counted against them. By definition they are temporary purchases. Once maternity clothes become necessary, they do not fit for long, and some women can hardly wait to outgrow them. The best thing that can be said about many such garments is that they are comfortable. The next best is that they do not look that bad. Occasionally a woman needs to buy new a maternity costume just for an occasion, to wear to a wedding or a party for which something she already owns will not suit now that she has become large. Stretchy clothes get worn and worn until the newly delivered woman is able to husk them off like snakeskin.

And then stuff them into a big trashbag. The solution to dressing oneself when pregnant usually is not a shopping spree, though many women will shop for particular items and may even enjoy some of them. Renting is an option for some. Even better, though, many pregnant women often find themselves welcomed into a network of short-term loans. While not all love their maternity clothes, maternity clothes become a way to communicate love, literally to embody it. Friends, sisters, neighbors, cousins, or coworkers noticing a pregnancy may offer items from their maternity wardrobes. The supply of these is ready for a range of reasons. No one's closet space is unlimited, and a woman not using these items for a while might be glad to share them with one who needs them. The garments acquire value when worn by one woman in an important phase of life and then shared with another. The assembling and delivering of maternity clothes to another woman in need of them is a corporal work of mercy. The recipient puts on these honored garments, even if they are not inherently glamorous, as vestments of sorts. When the borrower is done with them, maternity clothes usually get given back to the original owner or passed along to someone else.[12]

The shared experience of maternity can make women attentive to the needs, comforts, and discomforts of the period. This shared-experience approach can prove helpful not only with wardrobes but also with prenatal care itself. "Centering Pregnancy" is a care system that may enhance the time women spend with their medical provider and, importantly, with other women. OB practices using this approach vary its operation, but some trends are common. "Centering Pregnancy" appointments occur in a group. About eight to ten women with babies due around the same time, plus those who accompany them to help, may meet together. Each woman receives individual attention from doctors or nurses and then the group gathers to address common concerns. These group appointments allow contact with others in similar situations, an important aspect of this prenatal care. "We are meant to be in conversation with one another," the Centering home page advises, members of the groups "connected in ways not possible with traditional care." The system invites those who may be most attentive to this period to observe and assist each other through it. Their collaboration may give others outside a way to stand alongside it.[13]

These gestures—parties, clothing exchanges, mutual maternity appointments—help sketch out a few outlines of what might be done better. They are valuable to the extent that they already have some currency. Revival and adaptation of a few old practices in honor of a birthing woman might be counted too.

Delivering meals to families with new babies is usually a welcome gesture. I have delivered them in the past. But I did not realize how big a deal this was until it was done for me after the arrival of my middle child. Need had been less acute after my first birth. Before the birth of my first daughter I had stockpiled supplies in my freezer and pantry. My omnicompetent mother came soon after this granddaughter's arrival and made all things well. A neighbor, an excellent cook, left dinner on the kitchen island one summer afternoon while I was nursing in the bedroom. The dessert she left, a fruit tart and an enamel bowl full of blueberries the size of grapes, got folded into the mythology of my eldest's charmed infancy. New-mother meals were fine then, but I did not actually need them. I needed them after the second child came. Exhausted, I grabbed at those dropped-off containers of soup or casserole as at a lifeline. Now, whenever sign-ups for dinner deliveries for new-baby households come around, I sign up. I got good at showing up with a neat paper grocery bag layered with hot foods, cold foods, a fresh loaf, and something for dessert. It seemed impressive for a while.

But my bagged suppers have no *sprezzatura* at all, I realized when I was standing one day in an art museum in front of a wall-mounted *desco da parto*. In Renaissance Italy, among a population recovering from medieval plagues, affluent families embraced an art form known as the *desco da parto*, a special painted birth platter or tray. One side of these festive platters, often round, feature something at least vaguely birth-related, a literary scene or the birth of a saint or an image of infants. On the other can be found some adornment or amusement, like a chess or backgammon board. These trays had special purpose. They would be borne into the birth chamber with necessities for the newly delivered woman and those attending her. These *deschi* (*desco* in plural) could be important as gifts and were set apart for long use in the household. Lest the *desco* be sidelined as a minor piece of decorative art, it is worth noting that estimable painters of the Italian Renaissance devoted their skills to these. When the magnificent Florentine Lorenzo de Medici died, the *desco* received by his mother on the occasion of his birth was still hanging on his wall. *Deschi* were given in honor of a birth but they were directed to and for the birthing woman, not just the newborn.[14]

How much better it would be to bring a meal to a new-baby household on a *desco da parto* rather than in a grocery bag! Passing food on special platters need not be overdone. Postpartum households need lots of meals but one *desco* per baby would be plenty. Platters could be presented as friends' or family's gift to the newly delivered woman, an expression of support from those in relationship with her. Later, the *desco* could take its place as an everyday piece used at the family table. Inventories from Renaissance Italy indicate that some *deschi* got this kind of hard (loving) use. The platter could just as well be saved for rarer occasions, like a household's good dishes or cloth napkins. Birthdays would be obvious occasions for hauling out the *desco*, marking the event of this unique shared experience of woman and child.


**Bring in a Platter of Postpartum Cocktails**


At this writing, if you like the idea of a *desco da parto* to mark a friend's childbearing, you have to make your own. I have found no potter featured in online or brick-and-mortar shops who offers them to American buyers. But there are lots of good potters out there.

One function of this special birth platter, as testified by images of them in art, was for bringing the new mother a drink. Women delivering babies in American hospitals usually are denied most food and drink during labor, to keep the patient ready for the event of anesthesia. In any case, after delivery, first embrace, cord cutting, and episiotomy repair, offers of nourishment are usually welcome. Nurses or birth attendants might offer the newly delivered woman water or juice for refreshment while she waits for something more substantial.

That slurry of apple juice and ice chips can hit the spot. But the pages of old midwifery manuals give recipes for much more interesting beverages after delivery. In the "practical physick" section of his guide for midwives, Nicholas Culpeper recommended some drinks for women after birth. Depending on their condition, postpartum women could be given "thin wine," or assistants could blend "Cinnamon a dram, saffron a scruple," with other powders in water for the new mother to drink, or they could offer a "Decoction of Barley, Syrup, and Honey of Roses." To be sure, this writer was not exactly ordering up a round of mixed drinks for the new mother and her girlfriends, though it was not unusual for postpartum drinks to contain wine. The beverages did aim to restore, relax, invigorate the woman and her friends after long, hard work. Lying-in gatherings would occur for days after a birth. If the mother and baby both passed through birth alive and intact, there was plenty to celebrate. Lying-in celebrations traditionally included only women in keeping with the modesty that excluded most men from birth. Those who labored together were to feast together.[15]

There is much to be said for the midwife's model of care, for birth centers, for home births. But I suspect that when people who have never done it speak fondly about social childbirth and how desirable it would be, this is what they have in mind. Most American women have little actual experience with it. Most have not sat at a friend's bedside passing around drinks after helping with labor. The primary yearning given voice when some pine for this may not be first for un-medicated labor, but for the company of female friends rather than hospital personnel in scrubs, for relieved celebration rather than vital-signs monitoring.[16]

Sharing a feast with a woman who has completed pregnancy is a way that guests show such a feast is deserved. That is a good way to begin to think about how a community might pay due respect to this thing happening in its midst. The practice of supplying women with adequate and celebratory food and drink when they deliver babies could become universal, even de rigeur, like cake for birthdays. People could supply childcare and household help while the woman rests after birth. Key here is that we learn to be ready to offer these things because we agree they should be offered, not to wait for a birthing woman to have to request them out of desperation. *This* is what we do when someone is going to have a baby. Giving recognition to the woman's nurture rather than only to a newborn's arrival is important too when pregnancies do not end as hoped. A woman's doings on behalf of the fetus still constitute care given when the outcome is not a healthy baby but a stillbirth or miscarriage. Having in place regular ways to pay regard to pregnancy supplies something ready for hard occasions that arise too. Encouraging some kinds of broadly accepted gestures to honor pregnancy not only would help women on the receiving end, but would help to remind others of their significance.[17]

### Nurturing the Nurturer

In hospitals at night after the birth of each of my children I resented frequent visitations of the blood-pressure cuff and the thermometer, the rude intrusion of bright light from the hallway. But forced awake by measurements of blood or urine, I had time to sit alone with the fact that I had just done something colossal. It was satisfying to be finished with the doing. I felt entitled to rest, entitled to close the curtains and close my eyes because nothing else appropriately should be asked of me for a while after I had done all that. Saying that may sound ridiculous. Many women around the globe do not have the luxury of rest after birth. But they ought. Opportunity for rest is one indispensable baby gift, one never unwelcome in duplicates or for births after the first, a way of demonstrating respect for the work of bearing and birthing.

This is an important piece of childbirth tradition to reclaim. Providing postpartum nurture, attendance, baby help, and restorative food and drink does not require the invention of a new tradition and is almost always welcome. Not only culture but medicine indicates its importance. Recent studies of postpartum crises can instruct on this count. A 2016 project by ProPublica and NPR researchers traced the disturbing rise of maternal mortality in the United States to lapses in care for the birthing woman. Studies of African American women in 2017 and 2018 suggest that the stresses of life before birth can endanger both mother and baby at birth, and attentive treatment to women in pregnancy can make the difference between life and death. Of course, nobody means for a birthing woman to suffer under hospital care. But researchers find that sometimes the woman's health meets neglect while medical personnel focus on baby. Shocking incidents of apparently healthy, twenty-first-century American mothers dying in childbirth arise from a kind of forgetfulness about how serious a thing the woman is doing in bearing and birthing. Under the reassuring mantle of hospital procedures, we might make the mistake of thinking that birth has become no big deal.[18]

Special nurture for the birthing woman features in advice for treating postpartum depression, as it does for postpartum emergencies. Medication and counseling certainly have roles in treating postpartum depression. But the Mayo Clinic's suggestions for affected women emphasize these much less than works of care. To the woman it acknowledges, "You may feel less attractive, struggle with your sense of identity or feel that you've lost control over your life. . . . Remember, the best way to take care of your baby is to take care of yourself." Although articulated in terms of things a woman can do for herself, much advice for managing postpartum symptoms demands the presence and assistance of other people. Care offered to the postpartum woman is the reciprocal of her own unique caregiving in pregnancy: help given to her when she is strained by pregnancy and birth recognizes the singular position she has, that no one can give help to the fetus except through the woman.[19]

"Remember, the best way to take care of your baby is to take care of yourself." That bottom line of the Mayo Clinic's postpartum depression counsel may serve as a motto of prenatal care as a whole. On the grounds that the woman's actions could positively benefit the baby, reproductive health care providers learned to pay attention to a woman's well-being. The relationship between mother's health and baby's health always has been complex. Prenatal activities often put the woman to strenuous demands before—or without—clear assurance that following through with these requirements measurably benefit her baby. Does care for women in this experience have to be justified on grounds that it will make them more useful to someone else? This rhetoric of self-care makes nurture of the mother of a newborn seem like indulgence of immaturity, like babying of a woman who should behave maternally. Should a woman only be granted self-care so that she can give better service to this other person? The child needs, so the woman gives. That is the causal sequence we expect of her. We should expect more of ourselves in support.

The best way to care for baby may not, in fact, be for woman to take care of herself. It is tempting to suggest that having a postpartum doula become the new normal. But it would be better that we—neighbors, friends, family, colleagues—take part in the care of a newly delivered woman. Like maternity clothes, special care for a woman might prove useful both during and for a while after pregnancy. Much opportunity exists to do better. Humans have all kinds of ways besides money for designating persons or behaviors they think honorable. We honor athletes, actors, local heroes, celebrities, chefs, teachers, firefighters.

We give them medals, billboards, parades, cards, applause. Even when we give nothing, we keep in mind that what they have done should be counted as an impressive accomplishment. That would be a good start.

Jesus said the joy of a baby's arrival makes us forget the pain of birth, but it doesn't have to make us forget everything else. We should recognize the meaning for all of the fact that somebody did this for each of us. We live next to, work next to, somebody who is doing this even now. And we expect, the lot of us, that they will do it well, doing the things that have become part of common knowledge about what helps the person-to-be. We hope women will be willing to keep doing it. Of course women do not decide to get or stay pregnant in order to attract a pat on the back. A woman's labor to nurture and deliver a new life is not just her private project. That is what it takes, that there be people on earth.

## Delivering Pregnancy from Metaphor

During my first pregnancy, my husband's first book was on its way to publication. His academic mentor from Germany sent a letter of congratulations, lauding him on the anticipated births both of our actual child and of his book, his "geistiges Kind"—a phrase difficult to translate precisely, but approximately "brain child," the child of spirit or intellect.

The letter-writer is a kind person. He was congratulating us both. Still, his compliment grated. It echoed too much the old notion construing a baby as my husband's mental act coming to fruit in my gut. And even in a general sense, the metaphor of pregnancy just does not fit the publication of a book.

People use the metaphor all the time, sure, but it is rarely a good fit: a pregnant silence, a pregnant pause, a pregnant period. "What torments my heart suffered in mental pregnancy, what groans, my God!" Augustine cried out in his *Confessions*. Pregnancy is so significant and strange on its own, so encompassing and unpredictable a bodily event that its casual borrowing to describe something else is likelier to distort than explain. The fit is usually wrong, like a garment much too big or formal for the occasion. As an experience, pregnancy beggars metaphors. Metaphors may help describe pregnancy: bun in the oven, pea in the pod. But the other way around, pregnancy as a metaphor for something else, usually fails, or comes at cost of minimizing gestation.[20]

Rather than flattening someone else's experience of the process by which each of us arrived in life, we might have to concede the insufficiency of metaphor. Our very identity—in broad and narrow meanings of that word, what entitles us to claim a single and not a plural first-person pronoun—is that someone else engaged in a challenging physical labor in order that we would be. Carrying nascent life recalls our mortality, positioning women to stare it down and bring back the news to the rest of us. Pregnancy exhibits relationship as fundamental to human life. We call on each other to do well in order that the species go on, one adult body willing to carry, provide, protect, and suffer on behalf of another one not yet fully formed. In doing this work one has chances—available at other times too but available here in distinctive ways—to exercise some kinds of goodness. What a loss it would be to understand the point of this prenatal activity as just to get a baby born.

# Acknowledgments

One's mother and one's husband might be the first obvious people to thank in a book pondering the significance of pregnancy, and so they are, in ways to be detailed later. I owe thanks to many others too. I am grateful to the editors and staff at Eerdmans, especially David Bratt, Linda Bieze, Laura Hubers, and Suzanne Tibor. Colleagues and students at Gordon College and Valparaiso University helped refine ideas treated here. Jennifer Hevelone-Harper, Kirsten Heacock Sanders, Hilary Yancey, Libby Baker, Jill Karn, Chelsea Wagenaar, and Dorothy Bass have kept up these conversations over time. Debra Rienstra encouraged the project at key moments. Special thanks go to Elspeth Currie for her insight and manuscript assistance. My dear friend Christine Perrin has kept this vigil with me longest, and gratitude for her overflows. Congregations at Christ Church Hamilton/Wenham (MA) and Christ the Redeemer (Danvers, MA) helped me place childbearing in context of worship. Librarians provided essential help with research, especially Martha Crain at Gordon and Mark Robison at Valparaiso University.

Circling back to family, I wish I could say that my mother's stories of having five cesarean sections back when doctors recommended going no further than two— "If I had followed doctor's orders, you wouldn't be here!"—were what inspired my musings. My mother, Rose Sagan, is an astonishing person. If any gratitude can be piled on top of that due to the gift of existence and lifelong care, it must come for the example of her heroic courage. Next in line for appreciation are my children, Elle, Hannah, and Ben. It is so good that they are. The wonderful fact of their being anchors my abstractions about the value of bearing life. And finally, at start and finish of this chorus of thanks is my husband Tal. I thank him for his love and support.

# Notes

**CHAPTER 1**

1. Kayley Vernallis, "Of Courage Born: Reflections on Childbirth and Manly Courage," in Sarah LaChance Adams and Caroline R. Lundquist, eds., *Coming to Life: Philosophies of Pregnancy, Childbirth, and Mothering* (New York: Fordham University Press, 2013), 70.

2. Lisa Guenther, *The Gift of the Other: Levinas and the Politics of Reproduction* (Albany: State University of New York Press, 2006), 6; Florentien Verhage, "The Vision of the Artist/Mother: The Strange Creativity of Painting and Pregnancy," in Adams and Lundquist, *Coming to Life*, 311; Barbara Katz Rothman, *The Book of Life* (Boston: Beacon Press, 2001), 17.

3. Kevin Helliker, "Pregnant Women Get More Ultrasounds, without Clear Medical Need," *Wall Street Journal*, July 17, 2015.

4. Pregnancy guides are many. Fine analysis of these books comes in Laura Tropp, *A Womb with a View: America's Growing Public Interest in Pregnancy* (New York: Praeger, 2013), 36–46. Sallie Han summarizes practices in *Pregnancy in Practice: Expectation and Experience in the Contemporary US* (New York: Berghahn Books, 2015). See also Eugene Declercq et al., *Listening to Mothers III, Pregnancy and Birth: Report of the Third National US Survey of Women's Childbearing Experiences* (New York: Childbirth Connection, 2013), http://transform.childbirthconnection.org/reports/listeningtomothers/internet-use/). The *What to Expect When You're Expecting*

publishing empire maintains a website at http://www.whattoexpect.com /pregnancy/symptoms-and-solutions/landing.aspx.

5. Janelle S. Taylor, Linda L. Layne, and Danielle F. Wozniak, eds., *Consuming Motherhood* (New Brunswick, NJ: Rutgers University Press, 2004).

6. Updated data about American births, collected in part as a way of opposing excessive intervention in births and high rates of cesarean section, are published in http://www.birthbythenumbers.org/.

7. Kelly Oliver, *Knock Me Up, Knock Me Down: Images of Pregnancy in Hollywood Films* (Columbia University Press, 2012).

8. See Atul Gawande, "The Score: How Childbirth Went Industrial," *The New Yorker*, October 9, 2006; Jennifer Block, *Pushed: The Painful Truth about Childbirth and Modern Maternity Care* (New York: Da Capo Press, 2008); Robbie Davis-Floyd, *Birth as an American Rite of Passage*, 2nd. ed. (Berkeley: University of California Press, 2003); Wendy Simonds, Barbara Katz Rothman, and Bari Meltzer Norman, *Laboring On: Birth in Transition in the United States* (New York: Routledge, 2007). A classic feminist critique is Adrienne Rich, *Of Woman Born: Motherhood as Experience and Institution* (New York: Norton, 1995). Many women Pamela Klassen interviewed about home birth characterized it as a spiritual or religious experience. See Klassen, *Blessed Events: Religion and Home Birth in America* (Princeton: Princeton University Press, 2001), 66.

9. Michael Banner, *The Ethics of Everyday Life: Moral Theology, Social Anthropology, and the Imagination of the Human* (Oxford: Oxford University Press, 2014), 70.

10. James Mumford, *Ethics at the Beginning of Life: A Phenomenological Critique* (Oxford: Oxford University Press, 2013), 17, 22.

11. Anne Stensvold, *A History of Pregnancy in Christianity: From Original Sin to Contemporary Abortion Debates* (New York: Routledge, 2015), 12.

12. Tikva Frymer-Kensky, *Motherprayer: A Pregnant Woman's Spiritual Companion* (New York: Riverhead, 1996), xii–xiii.

13. Stensvold, *A History of Pregnancy*, 12; Susan Windley-Daoust, *Theology of the Body, Extended: The Spiritual Signs of Birth, Impairment, and Dying* (Hobe Sound, FL: Lectio Publishing, 2014), 33 (italics original for Windley-Daoust quotation); Frymer-Kensky, *Motherprayer*; Margaret L. Hammer, *Giving Birth: Reclaiming Biblical Metaphor for Pastoral Practice* (Louisville: Westminster/John Knox, 1994), 2, 9.

14. Stephanie Paulsell, *Honoring the Body: Meditations on a Christian Practice* (San Francisco: Jossey-Bass, 2002), 5–6; Windley-Daoust, *Theol-*

*ogy of the Body*, xi, 67. For an application of Christian principles to natural childbirth, see Helen Wessel, *The Joy of Natural Childbirth*, 5th ed. (Santa Rosa Beach, FL: Bookmates International, 1994).

15. Hammer, *Giving Birth*, 4–7; Windley-Daoust, *Theology of the Body*, 67; Rachel Marie Stone, *Birthing Hope* (Downers Grove, IL: Intervarsity Press, 2018).

16. See Maryanne Cline Horowitz, "The 'Science' of Embryology before the Discovery of the Ovum," in Marilyn J. Boxer and Jean H. Quataert, eds., *Connecting Spheres: European Women in a Globalizing World, 1500 to the Present*, 2nd ed. (New York: Oxford University Press, 2000); Clarissa Atkinson, chap. 2, "Physiological Motherhood," in *The Oldest Vocation: Christian Motherhood in the Middle Ages* (Ithaca, NY: Cornell University Press, 1991).

17. Donald Caton concurs in his study of changed attitudes toward obstetric anesthesia, *What a Blessing She Had Chloroform: The Medical and Social Responses to the Pain of Childbirth from 1800 to the Present* (New Haven: Yale University Press, 1999).

18. Kathleen Crowther-Heyck, "'Be Fruitful and Multiply': Genesis and Generation in Reformation Germany," *Renaissance Quarterly* 55, no. 3 (2002): 919–20. Sarah Knott gathers accounts of pregnancy in the past in *Mother Is a Verb: An Unconventional History* (New York: Sarah Crichton Books, 2019).

19. Irina Aristarkhova, *Hospitality of the Matrix: Philosophy, Biomedicine, and Culture* (New York: Columbia University Press, 2012), 52–57. I discovered this category problem firsthand when beginning this project. Rifling through indexes of books I thought must treat reproduction, I was baffled to find "Pregnancy" as a category usually missing from the index entirely. Relevant material turned out to be classified instead under "Embryo" or "Embryology."

CHAPTER 2

1. Kathleen A. Costigan, Heather L. Sipsma, and Janet A. DiPietro, "Pregnancy Folklore Revisited: The Case of Heartburn and Hair," *Birth: Issues in Perinatal Care* 33, no. 4 (2006): 311–14; Anahad O'Connor, "The Claim: Mother's Heartburn Means a Hairy Newborn," *New York Times*, February 20, 2007.

2. Costigan et al, "Pregnancy Folklore," 311–14.

3. Summaries of this history come in Tina Cassidy, *Birth: The Surprising History of How We Are Born* (New York: Atlantic Monthly Press, 2006); Randi Hutter Epstein, *Get Me Out: A History of Childbirth from the Garden of Eden to the Sperm Bank* (New York: Norton, 2011); and Edward Dolnick, *The Seeds of Life* (New York: Basic Books, 2017).

4. Maryanne Cline Horowitz, "The 'Science' of Embryology before the Discovery of the Ovum," in Marilyn J. Boxer and Jean H. Quataert, eds., *Connecting Spheres: European Women in a Globalizing World, 1500–Present* (New York: Oxford University Press, 1987), 110.

5. Ulinka Rublack, "Pregnancy, Childbirth, and the Female Body in Early Modern Germany," *Past and Present* 150 (1996): 108–10; Thomas Rogers Forbes, *The Midwife and the Witch* (New Haven: Yale University Press, 1966), viii–ix.

6. Stuart B. Blakely, "Superstitions in Obstetrics," *New York State Journal of Medicine* (1922): 117.

7. Monica H. Green calls *Der Swangern Frauwen und Hebammen Rosegarten* one of the most important works in the field for over a century and a half and imitated long after. "The Sources of Eucharius Rösslin's 'Rosegarden for Pregnant Women and Midwives' (1513)," *Medical History* 53, no. 2 (2009): 167–92.

8. Thomas Reynalde, *The Birth of Mankind, Otherwise Named, The Woman's Book* (1560), ed. Elaine Hobby (Farnham, UK: Ashgate, 2009), xvii; Clarissa Atkinson, *The Oldest Vocation: Christian Motherhood in the Middle Ages* (Ithaca, NY: Cornell University Press, 1991), 25–26; Mary E. Fissell, *Vernacular Bodies: The Politics of Reproduction in Early Modern England* (Oxford: Oxford University Press, 2005).

9. J. W. Ballantyne, *Expectant Motherhood: Its Supervision and Hygiene* (London: Cassell and Company, 1914), 51.

10. Atkinson, *The Oldest Vocation*, 29–31; Horowitz, "The 'Science' of Embryology," 104–5; Robert Barret, *A Companion for Midwives, Childbearing women, and nurses directing them how to perform their respective offices* (London: Tho. Ax, 1699), 44–45; Prudence Allen, RSM, *The Concept of Woman: The Early Humanist Reformation, 1250–1500* (Grand Rapids: Eerdmans, 2002). Aeschylus quoted in Mary Harlow and Ray Laurence, eds., *A Cultural History of Childhood and Family in Antiquity* (London: Bloomsbury Academic, 2012), 157–58.

11. Sophia M. Connell, "Aristotle and Galen on Sex Difference and

Reproduction: A New Approach to an Ancient Rivalry," *Studies in History and Philosophy of Science* 31, no. 3 (2000): 405–27; Thomas Laqueur, *Making Sex: Body and Gender from the Greeks to Freud* (Cambridge: Harvard University Press, 1990).

12. Atkinson, *The Oldest Vocation*, 25; Reynalde, *Birth of Mankind*, 51, 57–58.

13. See David Albert Jones, *The Soul of the Embryo: An Enquiry into the Status of the Human Embryo in the Christian Tradition* (London: Continuum, 2004), 131, 143, 148–50, 169–70.

14. Eve Keller, *Generating Bodies and Gendered Selves: The Rhetoric of Reproduction in Early Modern England* (Seattle: University of Washington Press, 2007), 68; Jacques Gélis, *History of Childbirth: Fertility, Pregnancy and Birth in Early Modern Europe* (Cambridge: Polity Press, 1991; reprint, 2005), 58.

15. Jones, *The Soul of the Embryo*, 19, 24, 50–52.

16. Jones, *The Soul of the Embryo*, 120.

17. Horowitz, "The 'Science' of Embryology," 108–9; Jones, *The Soul of the Embryo*, 166–67.

18. Atkinson, *The Oldest Vocation*, 40–41; Reynalde, *Birth of Mankind*, 39, 47.

19. Jones, *The Soul of the Embryo*, 161–62; Keller, *Generating Bodies*, 101, 106–8, 111–12.

20. The race to find sperm and egg is detailed in Matthew Cobb, *Generation: The Seventeenth Century Scientists Who Unraveled the Secrets of Sex, Life and Growth* (New York: Bloomsbury, 2006); Laqueur, *Making Sex*, 177–79.

21. Connell, "Aristotle and Galen," 421; Barret, *A Companion for Midwives*, 55; Jones, *The Soul of the Embryo*, 19, 24; Jane Sharp, *The Midwives Book* (1671), ed. Elaine Hobby (Oxford: Oxford University Press, 1999), 75.

22. Jones, *The Soul of the Embryo*, 22–25, 27; Gélis, *History of Childbirth*, 49.

23. Dante, *Purgatorio*, ed. and trans. Jean Hollander and Robert Hollander (New York: Anchor Books, 2004), Canto 25: 37–75.

24. Jones, *The Soul of the Embryo*, 113–15, 118–19, 122–23, 161–63, 172–73.

25. Jones, *The Soul of the Embryo*, 161; Reynalde, *Birth of Mankind*, 35; Nicholas Culpeper, *Directory for Midwives, or, a Book for Women* (London: Peter Cole and Edward Cole, 1662), 114–15.

26. Jones, *The Soul of the Embryo*, 166; Haller quoted in Horowitz,

"The 'Science' of Embryology," 109; Clara Pinto-Correia, *The Ovary of Eve: Egg and Sperm and Preformation* (Chicago: University of Chicago Press, 1997).

27. David Bainbridge, *Making Babies: The Science of Pregnancy* (Cambridge: Harvard University Press, 2001), 103–7.

28. Reynalde, *Birth of Mankind*, 23, 33.

29. Merry E. Wiesner-Hanks, *Women and Gender in Early Modern Europe*, 3rd ed. (Cambridge: Cambridge University Press, 2008), 84; Barret, *A Companion for Midwives*, 64; Mary E. Fissell, "Hairy Women and Naked Truths: Gender and the Politics of Knowledge in Aristotle's Masterpiece," *William and Mary Quarterly* 60, no. 1 (2003): 43–74; *Aristotle's Masterpiece* (New York, 1846), 11.

30. Gélis, *History of Childbirth*, 48, 147–49; John Sadler, *The Sicke Woman's Private Looking-Glasse Wherein Methodically Are Handled, All Uterine Affects or Diseases Arising from the Wombe* . . . (London, 1636), 142b, 146–47; *Aristotle's Masterpiece*, 113.

31. Sadler, *The Sicke Woman's Private Looking-Glasse*, 146; Culpeper, *Directory for Midwives*, 157.

32. Blakely, "Superstitions in Obstetrics," 117.

33. Laqueur, *Making Sex*, 59, 265; See also Cristina Mazzoni, *Maternal Impressions: Pregnancy and Childbirth in Literature and Theory* (Ithaca, NY: Cornell University Press, 2002).

34. J. W. Ballantyne, *Teratogenesis: An Inquiry into the Causes of Monstrosities* (Edinburgh: Oliver and Boyd, 1897), 31.

35. Philip K. Wilson, "'Out of Sight, Out of Mind?': The Daniel Turner-James Blondel Dispute over the Power of Maternal Imagination," *Annals of Science* 49, no. 1 (1992): 63–85; Rublack, "Pregnancy, Childbirth, and the Female Body," 95–97.

36. Julia Epstein, "The Pregnant Imagination, Fetal Rights, and Women's Bodies," *Yale Journal of Law & the Humanities* 7, no. 1 (1995): 154–55.

37. Culpeper, *Directory for Midwives*, 170–72; *Aristotle's Masterpiece*, 116; Keller, *Generating Bodies*, 118.

38. Fiona Harris Stoerz, "Midwives in the Middle Ages? Birth Attendants, 600–1300," in Wendy J. Turner and Sara M. Butler, eds., *Medicine and the Law in the Middle Ages* (Leiden: Brill, 2014), 65–66.

39. Wiesner-Hanks, *Women and Gender*, 83–91.

40. Reynalde, *Birth of Mankind*, 106; Jacqueline Marie Musacchio, *The*

*Art and Ritual of Childbirth in Renaissance Italy* (New Haven: Yale University Press, 1999).

41. Richard W. Wertz and Dorothy C. Wertz, *Lying In: A History of Childbirth in America,* expanded ed. (New Haven: Yale University Press, 1989), 31–34. See also Judith Walzer Leavitt, *Brought to Bed: Childbearing in America, 1750–1950,* reprint ed. (Oxford: Oxford University Press, 1988).

42. Lawrence D. Longo and Lawrence P. Reynolds, *Wombs with a View* (New York: Springer International, 2016), 184–85; Wertz and Wertz, *Lying In,* 39–43.

43. Green, "The Sources of Eucharius Rösslin's 'Rosegarden,'" 167–69.

44. Longo and Reynolds, *Wombs with a View,* 250–61; Katherine Phelps Walsh, against general assumption, suggests Sharp may have been a man. See Walsh, "Marketing Midwives in Seventeenth-Century London: A Re-examination of Jane Sharp's *The Midwives Book,*" *Gender & History* 26, no. 2 (2014), 223–41.

45. Harold Speert, *Obstetrics and Gynecology in America: A History* (Chicago: American College of Obstetricians and Gynecologists, 1980); Tanfer Emin Tunc, "The Mistress, the Midwife, and the Medical Doctor: Pregnancy and Childbirth on the Plantations of the Antebellum American South, 1800–1860," *Women's History Review* 19, no. 3 (2010): 395–419.

46. Wertz and Wertz, *Lying In,* 48, 65; Joseph DeLee, "Progress Towards Ideal Obstetrics," *American Journal of Obstetrics and Diseases of Women and Children* 73, no. 1 (January–June 1916): 407.

47. Donald Caton, *What a Blessing She Had Chloroform: The Medical and Social Response to the Pain of Childbirth from 1800 to the Present* (New Haven: Yale University Press, 1999); Irvine Loudon, *Death in Childbirth: An International Study of Maternal Care and Maternal Mortality, 1800–1950* (Oxford: Oxford University Press, 1992), 258–72; Culpeper, *Directory for Midwives,* 177.

48. Jacqueline H. Wolf, *Deliver Me from Pain: Anesthesia and Birth in America* (Baltimore: Johns Hopkins University Press, 2009), 23–26; Nicholson J. Eastman, *Expectant Motherhood,* 3rd ed. (Boston: Little, Brown, 1957), v.

49. Irvine Loudon, "The Tragedy of Puerperal Fever," *Health Libraries Review* 15 (1998), 151–56.

50. Wolf, *Deliver Me from Pain,* 111; Martha M. Eliot and Lillian R. Freedman, "Four Years of the EMIC Program," *Yale Journal of Biology and Medicine* 19 (1947): 621–35.

51. Lawrence D. Longo and Christina M. Thompsen, "Prenatal Care and Its Evolution in America," *Proceedings of the Second Motherhood Symposium* (Madison, WI: Women's Research Center, 1982), 29–70.

52. Eastman, *Expectant Motherhood*, v; Nicholson J. Eastman, "The Contributions of John Whitridge Williams to Obstetrics," *American Journal of Obstetrics and Gynecology* 90, no. 5 (1964): 561–65; Ballantyne, *Expectant Motherhood*, x–xiv, 33.

53. Ballantyne, *Expectant Motherhood*, xiv; Wolf, *Deliver Me from Pain*, 31.

54. Alice Bunker Stockham, *Tokology: A Book for Every Woman* (Chicago: Sanitary Publishing, 1885); Leo Wiener, ed. and trans., *The Complete Works of Leo Tolstoy*, vol. 20 (London: J. M. Dent, 1905), 499–500.

55. Marika Seigel, *The Rhetoric of Pregnancy* (Chicago: University of Chicago Press, 2013), 11; Ballantyne, *Expectant Mother*, v–vi.

56. Prudence B. Saur, *Maternity: A Book for Every Wife and Mother* (Chicago: L. P. Miller & Co., 1887); Carolyn Conant Van Blarcom, *Getting Ready to Be a Mother* (New York: Macmillan, 1925); S. Josephine Baker, *Healthy Mothers* (Boston: Little, Brown, 1920); Ornella Moscucci, "Holistic Obstetrics: The Origins of Natural Childbirth in Britain," *Postgrad Medical Journal* 79 (2003): 168–73; Minnie Randell, *Training for Childbirth*, 4th ed. (London: J&A Churchill, 1949); Cyril V. Pink, *The Foundations of Motherhood*, 4th ed. (London: Cassell, 1947).

57. Eastman, *Expectant Motherhood*; George A. Kelly, Robert J. Walsh, A. J. Vignec, and Robert P. Odenwald, *The Catholic Guide to Expectant Motherhood* (New York: Random House, 1961); Doris Hale Heinz and Katherine Smith Bolt, *Modeling for Motherhood: Heir Conditioning for the Modern Mrs.* (New York: Wiley, 1946).

58. *Prenatal Care* (Washington, DC: US Children's Bureau, 1913). The first edition was written by Mrs. Max West. Subsequent revisions were collaboratively authored by doctors, nurses, social workers, and policy makers.

**CHAPTER 3**

1. Anya Jabour, *Scarlett's Sisters: Young Women in the Old South* (Chapel Hill: University of North Carolina Press, 2007), 227.

2. In a 2002 PBS News report on the prenatal benefits of folic acid, the program's Judy Woodruff described the 1981 birth of her son, with spina

bifida: "I've come to understand now that it is believed that with the right amount of folic acid, you can . . . prevent up to 75 percent of babies with spina bifida. You can imagine how that makes you feel, to know that maybe there was something that you could have done that would have changed the life of your child and made him healthy. . . . I can't put it into words." "Folic Acid," *PBS Newshour Health*, August 19, 2002, http://www.pbs.org /newshour/show/folic-acid.

3. Michael F. Roizen and Mehmet C. Oz, *You: Having a Baby: The Owner's Manual to a Happy and Healthy Pregnancy* (New York: Simon & Schuster, 2009), 154–55; Doris Hale Heinz and Katherine Smith Bolt, *Modeling for Motherhood: Heir Conditioning for the Modern Mrs.* (New York: Wiley, 1946), 55. Heinz and Bolt call the doctor "Boss." See also Carolyn Conant Van Blarcom, *Getting Ready to Be a Mother* (New York: Macmillan, 1925), 9; Ellen Raymond, "I Worked Till My Baby Was Born," *Today's Woman* (January 1951), reprinted in Emanuel Greenberg, *Journey to Motherhood* (New York: St. Martin's Press, 1978), 49.

4. Raymond, "I Worked Till My Baby Was Born," 49.

5. Roizen and Oz, *You*, 7.

6. Gail Weiss, "Birthing Responsibility: A Phenomenological Perspective of the Moral Significance of Birth," in Sarah L. Adams and Caroline R. Lundquist, eds., *Coming to Life: Philosophies of Pregnancy, Childbirth, and Mothering* (New York: Fordham University Press, 2013), 116–17. Weiss points out that until birth, all care others may extend to the fetus is mediated through the mother, but upon delivery others may take up new responsibilities that the mother cannot.

7. Pope Pius XII, "Address to the Italian Association of Catholic Midwives," October 29, 1951; Robert P. Odenwald, "How to Maintain a Cheerful Attitude," in George A. Kelly, Robert J. Walsh, A. J. Vignec, and Robert P. Odenwald, *The Catholic Guide to Expectant Motherhood* (New York: Random House, 1961), 133.

8. Frances Gray, "Original Habitation: Pregnant Flesh as Absolute Hospitality," in Adams and Lundquist, *Coming to Life*, 85.

9. Van Blarcom, *Getting Ready*, 6–7.

10. Amy Laura Hall, *Conceiving Parenthood: American Protestantism and the Spirit of Reproduction* (Grand Rapids: Eerdmans, 2008), 253; Minnie Randell, *Training for Childbirth*, 4th ed. (London: J&A Churchill, 1949), vii; Vaughan, *Safe Childbirth*; Mario A. Castallo and Audrey Walz, *Expectantly Yours: A Book for Expectant Mothers and Prospective Fathers*

(New York: MacMillan, 1943), 15, 24; Cyril V. Pink, *The Foundations of Motherhood*, 4th ed. (London: Cassell, 1947), 15.

11. S. Josephine Baker, *Healthy Mothers* (Boston: Little, Brown, 1920), 111; L. Serene Jones, "Hope Deferred: Theological Reflections on Reproductive Loss (Infertility, Miscarriage, Stillbirth)," *Modern Theology* 17, no. 2 (April 2001): 233; Roizen and Oz, *You*, 155.

12. Lisa Guenther, *The Gift of the Other: Levinas and the Politics of Reproduction* (Albany: State University of New York Press, 2006), 31, 34–35. Janelle S. Taylor discusses some problems of considering pregnancy as work, a metaphor that comes from the dovetailing of industrial production and obstetric practice, in "Of Sonograms and Baby Prams: Prenatal Diagnosis, Pregnancy, and Consumption," *Feminist Studies* 26, no. 2 (2000): 393–418.

13. Raymond, "I Worked Till My Baby Was Born," 49–53.

14. Cristina Mazzoni, *Maternal Impressions: Pregnancy and Childbirth in Literature and Theory* (Ithaca, NY: Cornell University Press, 2002), 65; Minnie Randell, *Training for Childbirth*, 1; Nick Hopwood and Tatjana Buklijas emphasize that the tendency for women to think about the fetus this way is a recent development: "No eighteenth-century woman imagined an embryo developing inside her." See Hopwood and Buklijas, *Making Visible Embryos*. Online exhibit, 2008, http://www.sites.hps.cam .ac.uk/visibleembryos/.

15. Pink, *The Foundations of Motherhood*, 61.

16. Roizen and Oz, *You*, 154–55. Ilana Löwy traces how prenatal diagnosis magnifies worry in *Imperfect Pregnancies: A History of Birth Defects and Prenatal Diagnosis* (Baltimore: Johns Hopkins University Press, 2017).

17. Nicholson J. Eastman, *Expectant Motherhood*, 3rd ed. (Boston: Little, Brown, 1957), 49, 73.

18. Iris Marion Young, *On Female Body Experience: "Throwing Like a Girl" and Other Essays* (Oxford: Oxford University Press, 2005), 49.

19. James Mumford, *Ethics at the Beginning of Life: A Phenomenological Critique* (Oxford: Oxford University Press, 2013), 18, 109.

20. For history of ideas about ensoulment in Christian thought, see David Albert Jones, *The Soul of the Embryo: An Enquiry into the Status of the Human Embryo in the Christian Tradition* (London: Continuum, 2004). Especially useful here are chapters 2 (on Hippocrates and Aristotle) and chapters 6–8 (on antique and medieval Christian debates about ensoulment). For recent arguments occasioned by embryo experimentation, see

Robert P. George and Christopher Tollefson, *Embryo: A Defense of Human Life* (New York: Doubleday, 2008).

21. On these metaphors see Kathleen Crowther-Heyck, "'Be Fruitful and Multiply': Genesis and Generation in Reformation Germany," *Renaissance Quarterly* 55, no. 3 (2002): 915–17.

22. Barbara Katz Rothman, "Laboring Now," in Wendy Simonds, Barbara Katz Rothman, and Bari Meltzer Norman, *Laboring On: Birth in Transition in the United States* (New York: Routledge, 2007), 49.

23. "3-D Printed Ultrasound Lets Blind Mom 'See' Unborn Baby," CBS News, May 7, 2015, https://www.cbsnews.com/news/3d-printed -ultrasound-lets-blind-mom-see-unborn-baby/.

24. Rebecca Kukla, *Mass Hysteria: Medicine, Culture, and Mothers' Bodies* (Lanham, MD: Rowman and Littlefield, 2005), 108–9, 112–13.

25. Weiss, "Birthing Responsibility," 116–17.

26. Cynthia D. Coe, "Plato, Maternity, and Power: Can We Get a Different Midwife?," in Adams and Lundquist, *Coming to Life*, 32.

### CHAPTER 4

1. Stuart B. Blakely, "Superstitions in Obstetrics," *New York State Journal of Medicine* (1922): 117–18.

2. Lawrence D. Longo, *The Rise of Fetal and Neonatal Physiology: Basic Science to Clinical Care* (New York: Springer, 2013), 137–39.

3. Barbara Katz Rothman, *Recreating Motherhood: Ideology and Technology in a Patriarchal Society,* reprint ed. (New York: Norton, 1989; reprint, New Brunswick, NJ: Rutgers University Press, 2000), 58–61.

4. Leslie J. Reagan, *Dangerous Pregnancies: Mothers, Disabilities, and Abortion in America* (Berkeley: University of California Press, 2012); Agnes Howard, "From Rubella to Zika," *Commonweal* no. 31 (March 2016).

5. Cyril V. Pink, *The Foundations of Motherhood*, 4th ed. (London: Cassell, 1947), 15, 92, 102.

6. Doris Hale Heinz and Katherine Smith Bolt, *Modeling for Motherhood: Heir Conditioning for the Modern Mrs.* (New York: Wiley, 1946), 36–37; Laura E. Ettinger, *Nurse-Midwifery: The Birth of a New American Profession* (Columbus: Ohio State University Press, 2006), 37–38; Mario A.

Castallo and Audrey Walz, *Expectantly Yours: A Book for Expectant Mothers and Prospective Fathers* (New York: MacMillan, 1943), 14.

7. Heinz and Bolt, *Modeling for Motherhood*, 36–37, 41.

8. *Muller v. Oregon*, 208 US 412 (1908); Ruth Bader Ginsburg, "Muller v. Oregon: One Hundred Years Later," *Willamette Law Review* 45, no. 3 (2009): 359–80.

9. *Young v. United Parcel Service, Inc.*, 575 US (2015); Lara Grow, "Pregnancy Discrimination in the Wake of Young v. UPS," *University of Pennsylvania Journal of Law and Public Policy* 19, no. 2 (2016): 133–62; Natalie Kitroeff and Jessica Silver-Greenberg, "Pregnancy Discrimination Is Rampant inside America's Biggest Companies," *New York Times*, June 15, 2018.

10. Moises Velasquez-Manoff, "Should You Bring Your Unborn Baby to Work?" *The Atlantic*, March 2015; Minnie Randell, *Training for Childbirth*, 4th ed. (London: J&A Churchill, 1949), 40; Pink, *The Foundations of Motherhood*; Linda Villarosa, "Why America's Black Mothers and Babies Are in a Life-and-Death Crisis," *New York Times*, April 18, 2018.

11. Edwin Miller Fogel, *Beliefs and Superstitions of the Pennsylvania Germans* (Philadelphia: American Germanica Press, 1915), 353; Clare Hanson, *A Cultural History of Pregnancy: Pregnancy, Medicine, and Culture, 1750–2000* (Hampshire, UK: Palgrave Macmillan, 2004), 60–65; Susan C. Karant-Nunn, *The Reformation of Ritual: An Interpretation of Early Modern Germany* (New York: Routledge, 1997), 81, 83.

12. Karant-Nunn, *The Reformation of Ritual*, 78–87.

13. Thomas Rogers Forbes, *The Midwife and the Witch* (New Haven: Yale University Press, 1966), 88–91.

14. Michael K. Eshleman, "Diet during Pregnancy in the Sixteenth and Seventeenth Centuries," *Journal of the History of Medicine and Allied Sciences* 30, no. 1 (1975): 27.

15. Richard A. Meckel, *Save the Babies: American Public Health Reform and the Prevention of Infant Mortality, 1850–1929*, reprint ed. (Rochester, NY: University of Rochester Press, 2015).

16. *Prenatal Care* (Washington, DC: US Children's Bureau, 1913), 8–13, 19–20.

17. *Prenatal Care* (Washington, DC: US Children's Bureau, 1930), 6; *Prenatal Care* (Washington, DC: US Children's Bureau, 1949), 27; Pink, *The Foundations of Motherhood*, 40–41, 54, 102.

18. Nicholas Culpeper, *Directory for Midwives, or, a Book for Women* (London: Peter Cole and Edward Cole, 1662), 157–63.

19. Alice Bunker Stockham, *Tokology: A Book for Every Woman* (Chicago: Sanitary Publishing, 1885), 129; Pink, *The Foundations of Motherhood*, 39.

20. Eshleman, "Diet during Pregnancy," 26–27.

21. Ellen Raymond, "I Worked Till My Baby Was Born," *Today's Woman* (January 1951), reprinted in Emanuel Greenberg, *Journey to Motherhood* (New York: St. Martin's Press, 1978), 50–53; George A. Kelly, Robert J. Walsh, A. J. Vignec, and Robert P. Odenwald, *The Catholic Guide to Expectant Motherhood* (New York: Random House, 1961), 29.

22. Rothman, *Recreating Motherhood*, 60; Arlene Eisenberg, Heidi E. Murkoff, and Sandee E. Hathaway, *What to Expect When You're Expecting* (New York: Workman Publishing, 1996), 80–89.

23. Ulinka Rublack, "Pregnancy, Childbirth, and the Female Body in Early Modern Germany," *Past and Present* 150 (1996): 88–89.

24. Prudence B. Saur, *Maternity: A Book for Every Wife and Mother* (Chicago: L. P. Miller & Co., 1887), 174–75.

CHAPTER 5

1. Kayley Vernallis, "Of Courage Born: Reflections on Childbirth and Manly Courage," in Sarah LaChance Adams and Caroline R. Lundquist, eds., *Coming to Life: Philosophies of Pregnancy, Childbirth, and Mothering* (New York: Fordham University Press, 2013), 56, 67.

2. Michael Roizen and Mehmet Oz, *You: Having a Baby: The Owner's Manual to a Happy and Healthy Pregnancy* (New York: Simon & Schuster, 2009), 155.

3. *Catechism of the Catholic Church*, 1803; Aristotle, *Nicomachean Ethics*, trans. Terrence Irwin, 2nd ed. (Indianapolis: Hackett Publishing, 1999), 19; William C. Mattison III, *Introducing Moral Theology: True Happiness and the Virtues* (Grand Rapids: Brazos Press, 2008), 60–62; Richard J. Regan, ed., *Aquinas: The Cardinal Virtues* (Indianapolis: Hackett, 2005), vii–xii.

4. Vernallis, "Of Courage Born," 51.

5. Aristotle, *Nicomachean Ethics*, 89.

6. Josef Pieper, *Faith, Hope, Love*, revised ed. (San Francisco: Ignatius Press, 1997), 164.

7. John Paul II, *The Theology of the Body: Human Love in the Divine*

*Plan* (Chicago: Pauline Press, 1997). On the error of taking for granted this gift, Lisa Guenther argues, "The generosity of giving birth requires a situation in which it is not already demanded of women as their biological duty, and women's bodies are not reduced to mere vessels for reproduction or incubators for social property." Lisa Guenther, *The Gift of the Other: Levinas and the Politics of Reproduction* (Albany: State University of New York Press, 2006), 8; Virginia Woolf, *The Death of the Moth and Other Essays* (New York: Harcourt Brace, 1942), 237.

8. American Child Health Association, "The Expectant Mother in the House of Health" (New York: American Child Health Association, 1924), 2.

9. See Guenther, *Gift of the Other*, 115–19.

10. Ellen Raymond, "I Worked Till My Baby Was Born," *Today's Woman* (January 1951), reprinted in Emanuel Greenberg, *Journey to Motherhood* (New York: St. Martin's Press, 1978), 50–53; Bernarr Macfadden, *Preparing for Motherhood* (New York: Macfadden, 1930), 70.

11. Emily Oster, *Expecting Better: Why the Conventional Pregnancy Wisdom Is Wrong—And What You Really Need to Know* (New York: Penguin, 2014). "Drinking Safely during Pregnancy" is a promise featured on the front cover.

12. Jacques Gélis, *History of Childbirth: Fertility, Pregnancy and Birth in Early Modern Europe* (Cambridge: Polity Press, 1991; reprint, 2005), 85; Robert J. Walsh, "Your Care in Pregnancy," in George A. Kelly, Robert J. Walsh, A. J. Vignec, and Robert P. Odenwald, *The Catholic Guide to Expectant Motherhood* (New York: Random House, 1961), 43–44. Walsh endorses the periods of abstinence in the first and last six weeks plus on the days a woman would have had second and third periods.

13. James Brundage, *Law, Sex, and Christian Society in Medieval Europe* (Chicago: University of Chicago Press, 2009), 91–92; S. Josephine Baker, *Healthy Mothers* (Boston: Little, Brown, 1920), 87–89.

14. Alice Bunker Stockham, *Tokology: A Book for Every Woman* (Chicago: Sanitary Publishing Company, 1883), 137, 146–49; Baker, *Healthy Mothers*, 88–89.

15. Sickness language is common. See Jan Lewis and Kenneth A. Lockridge's article, "'Sally Has Been Sick': Pregnancy and Family Limitation among Virginia Gentry Women, 1780–1830," *Journal of Social History* 22, no. 1 (Autumn 1988), 5–19; Tanfer Emin Tunc, "The Mistress, the Midwife, and the Medical Doctor: Pregnancy and Childbirth on the Plantations

of the Antebellum American South, 1800–1860," *Women's History Review* 19, no. 3 (June 2010), 395–419; and Anya Jabour, *Scarlett's Sisters: Young Women in the Old South* (Chapel Hill: University of North Carolina Press, 2007), 223; 1950 woman quoted in Barbara Clow, "'An Illness of Nine Months' Duration': Pregnancy and Thalidomide Use in Canada and the United States," in Georgina Feldberg, Molly Ladd-Taylor, and Alison Li, eds., *Women, Health, and Nation: Canada and the United States since 1945* (Montreal: McGill-Queen's University Press, 2003), 54–55.

16. Barbara Katz Rothman, "Laboring Now," in Wendy Simons, Barbara Katz Rothman, and Bari Meltzer Norman, *Laboring On: Birth in Transition in the United States* (New York: Routledge, 2007), 48–49.

17. Leslie J. Reagan, *Dangerous Pregnancies: Mothers, Disabilities, and Abortions in Modern America* (Berkeley: University of California Press, 2012), 57–63.

18. Mauriceau quoted in Michael K. Eshleman, "Diet during Pregnancy in the Sixteenth and Seventeenth Centuries," *Journal of the History of Medicine and Allied Sciences* 30, no. 1 (1975): 29; Lisa Guenther, *The Gift of the Other: Levinas and the Politics of Reproduction* (Albany: State University of New York Press, 2006), 111, italics original. Sarah Jobe treats morning sickness and other symptoms as suffering in a Christian idiom in *Creating with God: The Holy Confusing Blessedness of Pregnancy* (Brewster, MA: Paraclete Press, 2011), 75–89.

19. Ziv Eisenberg, "Clear and Pregnant Danger: The Making of Prenatal Psychology in Mid-Twentieth-Century America," *Journal of Women's History* 22, no. 3 (Fall 2010): 112–35; Cyril V. Pink, *The Foundations of Motherhood*, 4th ed. (London: Cassell, 1947), 90.

20. Doris Hale Heinz and Katherine Smith Bolt, *Modeling for Motherhood: Heir Conditioning for the Modern Mrs.* (New York: Wiley, 1946), 2.

21. Sharon LaFraniere, "Nightmare for African Women: Birthing Injury and Little Help," *New York Times*, September 28, 2005.

22. Judith Walzer Leavitt, "Under the Shadow of Maternity: American Women's Responses to Death and Debility Fears in Nineteenth-Century Childbirth," *Feminist Studies*, 12, no. 1 (Spring 1986): 129–54, quotations from pp. 130 and 133; Patricia D. Suplee, Debra Bingham, and Lisa Kleppel, "Nurses' Knowledge and Teaching of Possible Postpartum Complications," *MCN: American Journal of Maternal Child Nursing*, August 2017 (*MCN in Advance* online), 1; Irvine Loudon, *Death in Childbirth: An Inter-*

*national Study of Maternal Care and Maternal Mortality, 1800–1950* (Oxford: Oxford University Press, 1992).

23. Giuliana Pelucchi, *Saint Gianna Berretta Molla: A Woman's Life* (Boston: Pauline Books, 2002); Pope John Paul II, "Canonization of Six New Saints." Homily for Sixth Sunday of Easter, May 16, 2004.

24. Frances Gray, "Original Habitation: Pregnant Flesh as Absolute Hospitality," in Sarah LaChance Adams and Caroline R. Lundquist, eds., *Coming to Life: Philosophies of Pregnancy, Childbirth, and Mothering* (New York: Fordham University Press, 2013), 71, 83.

25. Guenther, *Gift of the Other*, 101; Nicholson J. Eastman, *Expectant Motherhood*, 3rd ed. (Boston: Little, Brown, 1957), 22; Irina Aristarkhova, *Hospitality of the Matrix: Philosophy, Biomedicine, and Culture* (New York: Columbia University Press, 2012).

26. James Mumford, *Ethics at the Beginning of Life: A Phenomenological Critique* (Oxford: Oxford University Press, 2013), 22.

27. Kierkegaard quoted in Margaret L. Hammer, *Giving Birth: Reclaiming Biblical Metaphor for Pastoral Practice* (Louisville: Westminster/John Knox, 1994), 145.

28. Walsh, "Your Care in Pregnancy," 33.

29. Mumford, *Ethics at the Beginning of Life*, 105; Gray, "Original Habitation," 72. While a stranger, the fetus formed by one's sex cells and gestated in one's body is not entirely strange. Plenty of exceptions exist, especially in cases of donor sperm or egg, but commonly in pregnancy women can recognize the fetus as arising from some combination of their own physical stuff and acts.

30. Mumford, *Ethics at the Beginning of Life*, 106; Guenther, *Gift of the Other*, 111.

31. Timothy Fry, ed., *The Rule of St. Benedict*, reprint ed. (New York: Vintage Books, 1998), chapter 53; Jim Forest, *All Is Grace: A Biography of Dorothy Day* (Maryknoll, NY: Orbis Books, 2011); Susan Windley-Daoust, *Theology of the Body, Extended: The Spiritual Signs of Birth, Impairment, and Dying* (Hobe Sound, FL: Lectio Publishing, 2014), 76.

32. Gray, "Original Habitation," 84, 85.

33. Guenther, *Gift of the Other*, 6.

34. Vernallis, "Of Courage Born," 69–70.

35. Vernallis, "Of Courage Born," 70.

36. Thanks are due to Dorothy Bass, who helped develop ideas about

mortality as a fact of pregnancy. See also Vernallis, "Of Courage Born," 48, 57.

37. Jones offers, stunningly, an image of the Trinity, where at the death of Jesus "the living Godhead [held] death within it," as does a "woman who, in the grips of a stillbirth, has death inside her and yet does not die. . . . When Christ is crucified, God's own child dies." Jones is not equating women in such suffering with God or rendering this suffering "redemptive" but makes a "poetic move" that gives "a morphological space within which they might imagine God's solidarity with them as those who lose a future they had hoped for and who carry the weight of this loss inside them." L. Serene Jones, "Hope Deferred: Theological Reflections on Reproductive Loss," *Modern Theology* 17, no. 2 (2001): 235, 242.

38. Vernallis, "Of Courage Born," 65; Walsh, "Your Care in Pregnancy," 77–79.

39. C. H. Davis, "Childbirth: Primitive and Modern," *Surgery, Gynecology, and Obstetrics* 34 (1922): 636–41; "Painless Parturition" (anonymous), *The Boston Medical and Surgical Journal* (April 5, 1888): 356–57.

40. Vernallis, "Of Courage Born," 69; Windley-Daoust, *Theology of the Body*, 43–44.

41. Donald Caton, *What a Blessing She Had Chloroform: The Medical and Social Response to the Pain of Childbirth from 1800 to the Present* (New Haven: Yale University Press, 1999), ix, 90–107.

42. Hammer, *Giving Birth*, 134–38.

### CHAPTER 6

1. Lisa Guenther, *The Gift of the Other: Levinas and the Politics of Reproduction* (Albany: State University of New York Press, 2006), 78; Iris Marion Young, *On Female Body Experience: "Throwing Like a Girl" and Other Essays* (Oxford: Oxford University Press, 2005), 48.

2. Susan Windley-Daoust, *Theology of the Body, Extended: The Spiritual Signs of Birth, Impairment, and Dying* (Hobe Sound, FL: Lectio Publishing, 2014), 70.

3. Cynthia D. Coe, "Plato, Maternity, and Power: Can We Get a Different Midwife?," in Sarah LaChance Adams and Caroline R. Lundquist,

eds., *Coming to Life: Philosophies of Pregnancy, Childbirth, and Mothering* (New York: Fordham University Press, 2013), 34; Young, *On Female Body Experience*, 52.

4. The What to Expect website recommends, for those dark spots of pregnancy,"Might as well decide this is sexy!" http://www.whattoexpect .com/pregnancy/symptoms-and-solutions/chloasma.aspx.

5. Robert J. Walsh, "Your Care in Pregnancy," in George A. Kelly, Robert J. Walsh, A. J. Vignec, and Robert P. Odenwald, *The Catholic Guide to Expectant Motherhood* (New York: Random House, 1961), 47.

6. Nicholson J. Eastman, *Expectant Motherhood*, 3rd ed. (Boston: Little, Brown, 1957), 99.

7. Cyril V. Pink, *The Foundations of Motherhood*, 4th ed. (London: Cassell, 1947), 88.

8. Eastman, *Expectant Motherhood*, 40–42.

9. Leon Kass, *Toward a More Natural Science* (New York: Simon and Schuster, 2008), 48; Leon Kass, *Life, Liberty and the Defense of Dignity* (New York: Encounter Books, 2004), 101.

10. Kass, *Life, Liberty, and the Defense of Dignity*, 297; Coe, "Plato, Maternity, and Power," 32–33; Margaret Shea Gilbert, *Biography of the Unborn*. Reprint ed. (New York: Hafner, 1963), 80; Eastman, *Expectant Motherhood*, 32–33.

11. S. Josephine Baker, *Healthy Mothers* (Boston: Little, Brown, 1923), 47; Leslie Reagan, "From Hazard to Blessing to Tragedy: Representations of Miscarriage in Twentieth-Century America," *Feminist Studies* 29, no. 2 (2003): 356–78.

12. L. Serene Jones, "Hope Deferred: Theological Reflections on Reproductive Loss," *Modern Theology* 17, no. 2 (2001): 227–45.

13. Florentien Verhage, "The Vision of the Artist/Mother: The Strange Creativity of Painting and Pregnancy," in Adams and Lundquist, *Coming to Life*, 309.

14. Elizabeth Yuko, "When You Look Pregnant, but You're Not," *New York Times*, September 16, 2016, http://www.nytimes.com/2016/09/18 /well/family/when-you-look-pregnant-but-youre-not.html. Conversely, Odenwald scolds women whose embarrassment stems not from modesty but vanity: "In any event, there is no reason to feel that you must win a fashion show. You did not conceive your child to win a beauty contest." Odenwald, "How to Maintain a Cheerful Attitude," in *The Catholic Guide*, 133.

15. Ulinka Rublack, "Pregnancy, Childbirth, and the Female Body

in Early Modern Germany," *Past and Present* 150 (1996): 84–110; David Greene, "50 Years Later: Cokie Roberts on the 1968 Democratic Convention," Morning Edition, NPR, August 30, 2018.

16. Odenwald, "How to Maintain a Cheerful Attitude," 135; Michael Banner, *The Ethics of Everyday Life* (Oxford: Oxford University Press, 2014), 63.

17. "What a Neighbourhood" is the response of Gélis to antique texts describing the womb as "menacing." Jacques Gélis, *History of Childbirth: Fertility, Pregnancy and Birth in Early Modern Europe* (Cambridge: Polity Press, 1991; reprint, 2005), 58–59. The phrase is attributed to Augustine, quoted in Guenther, *The Gift of the Other*, 1.

18. Harold Speert, *Obstetrics and Gynaecology: History and Iconography*, 3rd ed. (New York: Parthenon Publishing, 2004), 175–79; Irina Aristarkhova, *Hospitality of the Matrix: Philosophy, Biomedicine, and Culture* (New York: Columbia University Press, 2012), 60–62.

19. Castallo and Walz, *Expectantly Yours*, 14.

20. This observation flows from French feminist Luce Irigaray's note of this fact's repression. See Coe, "Plato, Maternity, and Power," 33.

21. Mumford, *Ethics at the Beginning of Life*, 107; Guenther, *Gift of the Other*, 45; Aristarkhova, *Hospitality of the Matrix*, 47.

22. Barbara Katz Rothman, *Recreating Motherhood*, reprint ed. (New York: Norton, 1989; reprint, New Brunswick, NJ: Rutgers University Press, 2000), 57–67. See also Rothman, *The Book of Life* (Boston: Beacon Press, 2001), 16–17.

23. Alexandra Sifferlin, "Babies in Womb Prefer a Mother's Touch to Her Voice, Study Finds," *Time*, June 22, 2015; Viola Marx and Emese Nagy, "Fetal Behavioural Responses to Maternal Voice and Touch, *PLOS one*, June 8, 2015, http://journals.plos.org/plosone/article?id=10.1371/journal.pone.0129118; Gélis, *History of Childbirth*, 53.

24. Haptonomy, http://haptonomy.co.uk/; William D. Virtue, *Mother and Infant: The Moral Theology of Motherhood* (Rome: Pontificia Studiorium Universitas, 1995).

25. Verhage, "The Vision of the Artist/Mother," 314–15; Windley-Daoust, *Theology of the Body*, 73, 76; Aristarkhova, *Hospitality of the Matrix*, 46.

26. Prudence B. Saur, *Maternity: A Book for Every Wife and Mother* (Chicago: L.P. Miller & Co.: 1887), 160–61, 192–93. A late holdout for maternal impressions, Saur flips conventional assumptions, giving men

credit for providing the physical parts of the baby and women credit for the mental and spiritual.

27. Bernarr Macfadden, *Preparing for Motherhood* (New York: Macfadden, 1930), 48–49. Stressing the absurdity of maternal impressions, which he names "telepathy," Mcfadden suggests believers might as well believe women keep on doing this throughout the child's life; "Why should she not go on telepathing after the child is born, either mark it with deformities or give it good health and genius by wishing hard about such things?"

28. Van Blarcom, *Getting Ready to Be a Mother*, 128.

29. Amy M. Boddy, Angelo Fortunato, Melissa Wilson Sayres, and Athena Aktipis, "Fetal Microchimerism and Maternal Health: A Review and Evolutionary Analysis of Cooperation and Conflict beyond the Womb," *BioEssays* 37, no. 10 (October 2015): 1106–18.

### CONCLUSION

1. Russell Shorto, "No Babies?" *New York Times Magazine,* June 29, 2008.

2. Steven Lee Myers and Olivia Mitchell Ryan, "Once Strict on Births, China Races for a Boom," *New York Times*, August 12, 2018; Victoria Williams, *Celebrating Life Customs around the World: From Baby Showers to Funerals* (Santa Barbara, CA: ABC-CLIO, 2017), 72–74.

3. Gaia Pianigiani, "Italy's 'Fertility Day' Call to Make Babies Arouses Anger, Not Ardor," *New York Times*, September 13, 2016.

4. Helen Blackman, "Reproduction since 1750," in *The Routledge History of Sex and the Body, 1500 to the Present*, ed. Sarah Toulalan and Kate Fisher (London: Routledge, 2013), 372–76.

5. Robbie Davis-Floyd, *Birth as an American Rite of Passage*, 2nd ed. (Berkeley: University of California Press, 2004).

6. Adele Blankfield, "The Origins and Purposes of Antenatal Preparation," *The Australian Journal of Physiotherapy* 13, no. 1 (March 1967): 18–21.

7. Blankfield, "The Origins and Purposes," 20–21.

8. Williams, *Celebrating Life Customs*, 49–51.

9. Williams, *Celebrating Life Customs*, 22–24; Janelle S. Taylor, "Of Sonograms and Baby Prams: Prenatal Diagnosis, Pregnancy, and Consumption," *Feminist Studies* 26, no. 2 (2000): 391–418.

10. Debra Rienstra, *Great with Child: On Faith, Fullness, and Becom-*

*ing a Mother* (New York: Tarcher/Putnam, 2002), 136–37; Tikva Frymer-Kensky, *Motherprayer: A Pregnant Woman's Spiritual Companion* (New York: Riverhead, 1996), 168–71.

11. Richard W. Wertz and Dorothy C. Wertz, *Lying In: A History of Childbirth in America*, expanded ed. (New Haven: Yale University Press, 1989), 3; Kay Goldman, *Dressing Modern Maternity: The Frankfurt Sisters of Dallas and the Page Boy Label* (Lubbock, TX: Texas Tech University Press, 2013).

12. Nicky Gregson and Vikki Beale, "Wardrobe Matters: The Sorting, Displacement, and Circulation of Women's Clothing," *Geoforum* 35, no. 6 (November 2004): 689–700. Thanks to Dorothy Bass for insights about the meaning of sharing these garments.

13. Centering Pregnancy website, https://www.centeringhealthcare.org/what-we-do/centering-pregnancy.

14. Jacqueline Marie Musacchio, *The Art and Ritual of Childbirth in Renaissance Italy* (New Haven: Yale University Press, 1999), 76–78.

15. Nicholas Culpeper, *Directory for Midwives, or, a Book for Women* (London: Peter Cole and Edward Cole, 1662), 187–97.

16. Wertz and Wertz, *Lying In*, 3.

17. Susan Starr Sered, "Husbands, Wives, and Childbirth Rituals," *Ethos* 22, no. 2 (1994): 188.

18. Nina Martin and Renee Montagne, "The Last Person You'd Expect to Die in Childbirth," *ProPublica*, May 12, 2017; Linda Villarosa, "Why America's Black Mothers and Babies Are in a Life-or-Death Crisis," *New York Times Magazine*, April 11, 2018.

19. "Postpartum Depression, Diagnosis & Treatment," Mayo Clinic, https://www.mayoclinic.org/diseases-conditions/postpartum-depression/diagnosis-treatment/drc-20376623.

20. St. Augustine, *Confessions*, trans. Henry Chadwick (Oxford: Oxford University Press, 2008), 120; Cynthia D. Coe, "Plato, Maternity, and Power: Can We Get a Different Midwife?," in Sarah LaChance Adams and Caroline R. Lundquist, eds., *Coming to Life: Philosophies of Pregnancy, Childbirth, and Mothering* (New York: Fordham University Press, 2013), 32.

# Select Bibliography

Much worthy writing exists on pregnancy and related topics. For specialized interests and primary sources, I direct readers to the more extensive information in endnotes. The books selected below, all secondary sources, are well suited for further reading in history, philosophy, and culture connected to childbearing.

Adams, Sarah LaChance, and Caroline R. Lundquist. *Coming to Life: Philosophies of Pregnancy, Childbirth, and Mothering*. New York: Fordham University Press, 2013.

Cassidy, Tina. *Birth: The Surprising History of How We Are Born*. New York: Atlantic Monthly Press, 2006.

Caton, Donald. *What a Blessing She Had Chloroform: The Medical and Social Response to the Pain of Childbirth from 1800 to the Present*. New Haven: Yale University Press, 1999.

Davis-Floyd, Robbie. *Birth as an American Rite of Passage*. 2nd ed. Berkeley: University of California Press, 2004.

Dolnick, Edward. *The Seeds of Life*. New York: Basic Books, 2017.

Epstein, Randi Hutter. *Get Me Out: A History of Childbirth from the Garden of Eden to the Sperm Bank*. New York: Norton, 2011.

Fissell, Mary E. *Vernacular Bodies: The Politics of Reproduction in Early Modern England*. Oxford: Oxford University Press, 2004.

Frymer-Kensky, Tikva. *Motherprayer: A Pregnant Woman's Spiritual Companion*. New York: Riverhead, 1996.

Gélis, Jacques. *History of Childbirth: Fertility, Pregnancy, and Birth in Early Modern Europe*. Reprint ed. Cambridge: Polity Press, 2005.

Hammer, Margaret L. *Giving Birth: Reclaiming Biblical Metaphor for Pastoral Practice*. Louisville: Westminster/John Knox, 1994.

Han, Sallie. *Pregnancy in Practice: Expectation and Experience in the Contemporary US*. New York: Berghahn Books, 2015.

Hanson, Clare. *A Cultural History of Pregnancy: Pregnancy, Medicine and Culture, 1750-2000*. Hampshire, UK: Palgrave-Macmillan, 2004.

Jobe, Sarah. *Creating with God: The Holy Confusing Blessedness of Pregnancy*. Brewster, MA: Paraclete Press, 2011.

Jones, David Albert. *The Soul of the Embryo: An Inquiry into the Status of the Human Embryo in the Christian Tradition*. London: Continuum, 2004.

Keller, Eve. *Generating Bodies and Gendered Selves: The Rhetoric of Reproduction in Early Modern England*. Seattle: University of Washington Press, 2007.

Klassen, Pamela. *Blessed Events: Religion and Home Birth in America*. Princeton: Princeton University Press, 2001.

Leavitt, Judith Walzer. *Brought to Bed: Childbearing in America, 1750–1950*. Reprint ed. Oxford: Oxford University Press, 1988.

Longo, Lawrence D., and Lawrence P. Reynolds. *Wombs with a View: Illustrations of the Gravid Uterus from the Renaissance through the Nineteenth Century*. New York: Springer, 2016.

Mazzoni, Cristina. *Maternal Impressions: Pregnancy and Childbirth in Literature and Theory*. Ithaca, NY: Cornell University Press, 2002.

Mumford, James. *Ethics at the Beginning of Life: A Phenomenological Critique*. Oxford: Oxford University Press, 2013.

Pinto-Correia, Clara. *The Ovary of Eve: Egg and Sperm and Preformation*. Chicago: University of Chicago Press, 1997.

Rothman, Barbara Katz. *Recreating Motherhood: Ideology and Technology in a Patriarchal Society*. Reprint ed. New Brunswick, NJ: Rutgers University Press, 2000.

Schaffir, Jonathan. *What to Believe When You're Expecting: A New Look at Old Wives' Tales in Pregnancy*. New York: Rowman & Littlefield, 2017.

Stensvold, Anne. *A History of Pregnancy in Christianity: From Original Sin to Contemporary Abortion Debates*. New York: Routledge, 2015.

Taylor, Janelle, S., Linda L. Layne, and Danielle Wozniak, eds. *Consuming Motherhood*. New Brunswick, NJ: Rutgers University Press, 2004.

Wertz, Richard W., and Dorothy C. Wertz. *Lying In: A History of Childbearing in America*. Expanded ed. New Haven: Yale University Press, 1989.

Windley-Daoust, Susan. *Theology of the Body, Extended: The Spiritual Signs of Birth, Impairment, and Dying*. Hobe Sound, FL: Lectio Publishing, 2014.

Wolf, Jacqueline. *Deliver Me from Pain: Anesthesia & Birth in America*. Baltimore: Johns Hopkins University Press, 2009.

Young, Iris Marion. *On Female Body Experience: "Throwing Like a Girl" and Other Essays*. Oxford: Oxford University Press, 2005.

# Index